A guide to organising
the chaos and making time
for family fun

NICOLE AVERY

Wrightbooks

Dedicated to The Happy Birdcage

First published 2011 by Wrightbooks

an imprint of John Wiley & Sons Australia, Ltd

42 McDougall Street, Milton Qld 4064

Office also in Melbourne

Typeset in Palatino LT 11/14.2pt

© Nicole Avery 2011

The moral rights of the author have been asserted

National Library of Australia Cataloguing-in-Publication data:

Author:	Avery, Nicole.
Title:	Planning with kids: a guide to organising the chaos and making time for family fun / Nicole Avery.
ISBN:	9780730375647 (pbk.)
Notes:	Includes index.
Subjects:	Child rearing.
	Parenting.
Dewey number:	649.1

Cover design by Josh Durham <www.designbycommittee.com>

Cover images: Folders: © iStockphoto.com/emily2k. Dinosaur: © iStockphoto/Midhat Becar. Pencils: © iStockphoto/Mehmet Salih Guler. Notepad: SXC. Paper: Bigstock / © JohnDavidHenkel. Images in table 12.2: © Vector / © Nevena / © Vector / © Nikita Chisnikov/ © Miguel Angel Salinas Salinas / © Vector / © Vector / © Vector / © Vector / © kaadesigns / © Vector / © Nikolai Pozdeev/ © Vector / © Riverstudio / © Vector / © lineartestpilot. All images used under license from Shutterstock.

Part openers: © Janine Lamontagne / © Anthony Boulton / © RainforestAustralia / © michelle junior / © Kyu Oh / © Bart Broek / © Michael Flippo / © Alexander Kalina / / iStockphoto: © David Gunn / © Talaj / © Brandon Laufenberg / © ElementalImaging / © Shane White / © DNY59. All images © iStockphoto, except for woman's handbag with cosmetics © Selena used under licence from Shutterstock

Printed in Australia by Ligare Book Printer

10 9 8 7 6 5 4 3 2 1

Disclaimer

Contents

Acknowledgements

This book has been a team effort with roles played by family, friends and loyal readers of the blog. Love and thanks to my husband, Phil, who put me on the path to organisation and who believes in me, even when I don't. And to my five amazing kids, all completely different, who have all taught me ways to be a better mother.

Thanks to those dear friends and family who subscribed to my blog from the very beginning and encouraged me to keep going: Mum, Sam, Cass, Steph, Lesley, Janne and Murray, Ed, Cath, Tash, Carolyn, Paula, Catherine, Annie, Deb, Nic, Bree, Sim, Kerry, Belinda, Lou, Justine and Laine.

Writing this book has been my biggest organisational challenge by far and I had many fabulous people to help me with it. Thanks again to Phil, who took time off work and did stints as the primary carer so I could work on the manuscript. To the kids who adjusted so well to me being busier on weekends. Thank you very much also to those who helped out with school pick-ups, after-school activities and looking after the little ones to give me more time to write: Lou, Belinda, MC, Leona, Kate, Angela, Danielle, Peter and Cath. A special thanks to Karen, who generously gave her expert but practical advice throughout the writing process.

To the readers of <www.planningwithkids.com>, thank you so very, very much. The book wouldn't exist without you. Your loyal visits to the blog showed me that people wanted to read what I had written!

Included in the book are many planning-related quotes from readers of the blog, friends and family. Thank you for sharing your knowledge and allowing me to include your quotes. The book is certainly enhanced by their inclusion.

To Mary Masters, who saw the potential in the blog and helped move the *Planning with Kids* manuscript from a collection of blog posts to a well-defined book. To Georgie Way and Alice Berry, thank you for your enthusiasm, encouragement and championing of the book. And finally, to Sandra Balonyi, who did an amazing job of cutting out my waffle and making the book easier to read.

Introduction

As a parent, I use planning as a safety blanket. When the chaos of daily life engulfs me, it's the constant in my life that lets me weave my way through all the school runs, the after-school activities, the washing, the cooking and the cleaning required to keep family life ticking along.

Planning with Kids is based on my blog of the same name. It's not a parenting book; it's an organisational book that shares the plans and routines I've created to make family life more manageable. If you read the word 'planning' and shuddered because you don't think you're a natural planner, read on because I can give you hope!

When I explain to people that I wasn't always an organised person, they're often surprised. Believe it or not, I grew up as a dawdling, absentminded, tardy kid—a point often raised by my family and oldest of friends! It's also amusing that my eldest son is just like I was—forever forgetting school notes, easily straying from a task and oblivious to the exasperation he causes me. At least I know it's possible to grow out of disorganisation, because that's exactly what I did.

Before children

Originally a country girl, I moved to the city to attend university when I was 17. While I probably acquainted myself a little too much with the city nightlife initially, I did manage to successfully complete my studies and graduate with a Bachelor of Business (Finance).

I didn't have a plan for what I was going to do after university and I wasn't focused on a career, but I took the available opportunities within the large company I was working for and eventually found a job I enjoyed as a performance analyst. The role was primarily numbers-based, focusing on budgeting, improving productivity and reporting. It was here I learned about the power of spreadsheets!

The budgeting skills I was employing at work certainly weren't being transferred to home and I was living from pay to pay. However, I'd found my niche at work and progressed to manager level. Even with the extra responsibilities of my new role and the delegation, negotiation and time-management skills I was developing, not much was changing in my personal life. But it soon would.

My gorgeous husband-to-be, Phil (with whom I'd been going out for a year), was far more disciplined with spending than I and he encouraged me to start saving for an overseas holiday. Without his push I might have never left the country, and travelling on my own was certainly one of the best things I ever did. My return home turned out to be the highlight though, as Phil met me at the airport—dressed in a tuxedo—with a ring, and asked me to marry him.

Phil has been the most defining influence in my life and I credit him with teaching me how to get organised. I credit myself with helping him to take the less trodden path. We balanced each other out then just as we do now.

Then there was baby

We weren't one of those couples who conceive as soon as they start trying. It took more than six months and, in the process, I found a new application for spreadsheets. When we did become pregnant in 1997 we were very excited. However, being one of the first couples among our friends and siblings to have children, our exposure to babies was quite limited. Only when we took our beautiful boy home did I truly realise I had no idea how to look after a baby.

When my maternal child health nurse arrived for my first home visit 10 days later, I opened the door in tears. I still remember the day, her name (Liz) and how helpless I felt. While Liz helped me out with the initial adjustments, there were many more episodes of confusion, tears and self-doubt in my parenting. I loved my new mothering gig, but found the role challenging—babies don't always follow the rules!

Working versus staying at home

When I was pregnant with our first child, I made plans to return to work after three months. Within a week of having our baby, I knew I wouldn't want to go back to work that soon. Luckily for me, my boss understood and allowed me to change my plan and return to work when my baby was nine months old.

I did feel guilty going back to work, even though I knew it was the right thing to do for my family at the time. I worked for just over 18 months before I went on maternity leave again with our second child. At the end of my 12 months' maternity leave in 2002 I had to decide whether I wanted to return to work or remain at home.

For the last three months of my maternity leave I became obsessed with deciding what to do. I loved being home with the kids, but part of me was scared of letting go of my career. What would I tick in 'Occupation' boxes? And how would I tell people what I did?

In the end, I knew we wanted to have more children, and I wanted to be at home at this stage of their lives. I moved beyond issues of title, other people's opinions and, most importantly, my own fear.

Almost 10 years later I'm technically back in the workforce deriving an income from <www.planningwithkids.com> and I can control the hours I work around my family. There are moments when I wish I had more freedom (for example, going to the toilet on my own)—where I imagine myself walking out the door in the morning, reading the paper on the train, having a lunch break and spending full days away from the kids— but I know it isn't as simple as that. With working away from home comes the hassle of finding good childcare, the drop-offs and pick-ups, sick days, competing interests and worry.

If you're returning to work as a new parent or just thinking about how this could be done successfully, the tips and routines throughout the book can help you organise your daily workload so that getting out the door for work will be more manageable. Streamlining your everyday household jobs and getting the kids involved in the chores will ease your workload and decrease the morning rush-hour stress.

What I have learned through the 'working versus staying at home' dilemma is that whatever choice you make, it's important that you take happiness and wellbeing into account—not only the kids' and your partner's, but yours too. To take the best care of your family, you have to make sure you take care of yourself and are happy in what you're doing.

The beginning of my planning obsession

In growing our family of five children, the adjustment from one to two children was the hardest. Learning to cope with a newborn while having a toddler around was quite challenging, especially as the baby wouldn't sleep for more than 45 minutes during the day.

Throughout the first year of my second child's life, I often felt out of control and disorganised. It wasn't until I'd resigned from my job that I realised that to regain some sense of order and organisation I needed to apply the skills I'd used daily in the office to my family life. I couldn't plan all the things a baby or toddler would do during the day, but there was so much around the home that I could plan and prepare for.

This was a big moment for me. Being home fulltime was my new 'job' and, just as I would have done in my old job, I needed to find ways of improving the organisation of daily tasks. I'd made a shift from considering myself as not having a job to making my role as a mother my job, using all the skills I had to make life easier and more enjoyable for my family and myself. My first project was to get the evening meals under control as 5 pm had become a time of day that I dreaded. An overtired baby, a toddler wanting attention and a meal waiting to be prepared was a stressful and regular scenario.

It started out pretty small: I created a spreadsheet with all the meals I liked to cook and which the kids would eat. It listed each recipe, ingredients and instructions, and I could quickly generate a weekly shopping list of all the ingredients I needed for the week. No last-minute trips to the shops with children in tow as I had a comprehensive shopping list to work from. This single change to my routine made a significant difference to how I coped throughout the day. Most importantly, it increased my confidence in my own ability to be able to do my 'new job'. I couldn't make the baby go to sleep exactly when I wanted to or make him stay asleep once he'd finally nodded off, but I could easily plan and prepare for the evening meals.

My second project was to ensure I didn't become one-dimensional. Before I had children, I always had a number of interests outside of my work. I wanted to make sure that as a mum I could fit in time to enjoy interests outside of the home, so I set about doing this.

With the continuing support of my husband and two success-ful home projects, I had enough confidence in myself to know I'd not only cope with having more children, but I'd love it. And have more children we did! We're blessed to have five beautiful, happy, healthy kids with whom we live in a state of organised chaos. There is roughly a two-and-a-half-year gap between each child and the next in our family. Our eldest boy is 12, our second son nine, our only daughter seven, our third son four, and the baby of the family (a boy) is now two.

Planning the parenting journey

With each child I've learned more about how to be a mother and more about myself. As our family has grown I've read books, attended parenting seminars, listened to other parents and listened to my kids to help me find the best ways of managing daily family life. I've also developed strategies and processes to help me cope more ably with the workload that comes with a young family.

I consider parenting the most important job I am doing at the moment so it is essential to keep up to date, as in a paid job. This involves reading widely, and taking time out to assess discipline strategies, educational needs, family nutrition and so on.

Karen Comer, mum of three
<www.earthlyjoyride.blogspot.com>

What I share in this book is the by-product of trial and error over more than a decade. Don't think it all runs perfectly at our house, because that's certainly not the case. There are days when I can hardly wait for the kids' bedtime to come around so I can have five minutes of peace and quiet. There are tears and fights that could have been prevented if I'd responded to certain situations differently. And there are those days when it all seems to go horribly wrong. Two fantastic things about parenting are that children are very forgiving and there's always tomorrow. When I get it wrong, I apologise to the kids, and they move on pretty quickly. Sometimes I wish I could move on as quickly as they do.

At the time of writing, our eldest is only 12. We have yet to experience the joy of adolescence and the new territory this is sure to bring with it (sex, drugs and rock 'n' roll — eek!) and so our parenting journey will continue. I'll make more mistakes. I'll get frustrated, I'll cry and pull out more of my hair. But I'll also have immense fun, laugh loudly, shed tears of pride and joy, love fiercely and learn more about being a parent.

Sharing the journey

With our first child, I had very few experiences to draw upon for helping me look after him. With each new baby, I've had a new starting point to parent from. As the kids grew and I met more parents, I listened to their advice and benefited from their experiences. I too have begun to share my learning with other new parents as they ask about the practicalities of looking after young kids. In 2008 I took the sharing of my parenting journey to a new medium: <www.planningwithkids.com> was born.

I write several times a week under the moniker of PlanningQueen, sharing the family things we do in our daily life to make life a bit easier and leave more time for fun. The blog has brought me immense joy. Reading the feedback from readers on how the ideas from <www. planningwithkids.com> have helped them regain some order and calm in their homes gives me great satisfaction. Throughout the book you'll find some great planning quotes from readers of my blog.

This book has the same philosophy as the blog—plan for the things you can so you're better able to manage whatever else comes your way. It shares what has worked for my family and gives you tips on how to implement this in your home. With each child I've found new shortcuts and tricks and I always think, 'I wish I knew *that* when I was having my last child'. The information I share is not rocket science— it's only known from experience.

The book covers areas of life for a family with children aged 12 and under, as this is where I'm up to with my experience as a parent. Realistically, if you have children who are this age or older, you'll have established your own ways of organising the chaos and learned from your own mistakes! Not everything I write in this book will suit every family. Families are too diverse and dynamic for that to be the case. I'd encourage you to try new ideas and stick with those that fit your family.

As a parent I've found small changes to household practices can make a massive difference to the harmony and balance of life. I hope this book will help you discover new ideas to enhance your organisation and allow more time for parenting.

Part I
Organising your family

Chapter 1

Routines

Regular daily family life is full of repetitive and often boring chores. As our family has grown, I've learned a lot about being a parent and running a household. The most useful tip I've learned from my insight into parenthood has been to plan whatever you can so that when the unpredictable realities of family life arise they're much easier to cope with. This insight has been my main inspiration for creating simple routines and guidelines for managing our daily life. They've helped me to manage the high volume of repetitive household chores, and freed up time for more fun activities such as playing with the kids.

Establishing routines

Routines are like a comfort blanket for kids; they give them a sense of security. They let kids know what's coming up, what's expected of them and when it's expected, which helps to place boundaries around their big wide world.

Routines are so important for kids! As an early childhood teacher I could usually tell which students had become accustomed to predictable routines at home, and were used to being assigned regular jobs. These children often transitioned much more smoothly [in]to school!

Catherine Oehlman, mum of two
<www.squigglemum.com>

Routines don't have to incorporate every waking minute of the day, but it's helpful if they cover the key activities that take place in daily life. For example, on school days there needs to be a more specific routine to ensure no-one is late, while on weekends and during school holidays routines can act more as a fluid framework around which to organise your day.

The best way to develop a routine for your family is to consider these key factors:

- your children's natural preferences
- regular family activities.

For example, in our house the kids are early risers, and this can often mean I start my day at 5 am! Instead of viewing this as a cross to bear, I use it to my advantage to kickstart our daily routine. In families with young children, giving yourself plenty of time to prepare the kids and everything else for school makes the mornings less stressful.

Our early morning routine also suits the children's natural preferences. Two of my school-aged children have a leisurely approach to getting ready. They like to have time to read or play and take things slowly in the morning so they get up early. If they got up half an hour before we leave the house, our mornings would soon become a battleground, with time and leisure competing fiercely. My other school-aged child is very different. His priority is to get himself ready and to be organised. He loves getting to school as early as possible so he has time to play before the bell rings, and he hates being late. This works beautifully in my favour as he's willing to help me and work cooperatively with the other children to ensure we leave the house on time.

Like most families with school-aged children, during the school term we have a number of after-school activities. There are activities such as dance classes, swimming lessons and footy training sessions to schedule in, and they help determine our weekly routine. As these activities can change each term, our routine needs to be modified regularly.

Unavoidable necessities have also helped shape our family routines. For example, over the past 11 years I've spent more time breastfeeding than not; therefore, this has been a big factor in determining our daily routine. As my husband has always worked reasonably long hours, I've had to juggle the bulk of the evening routine on my own. This is not something I've always found easy. There was often a tired toddler wanting attention or a grizzly baby in need of a calming feed competing for my time.

About six months into life with our second child, I decided I could better manage the baby's last feed of the day if I allowed our then 2 and a half year old to have his TV time while I breastfed. This system worked beautifully. The 30 minutes during which our toddler watched his pre-recorded show of *Playschool* allowed me to calmly give the baby his last feed of the day. I could then spend time with our toddler reading stories quietly while the baby was sound asleep.

Morning and evening routines are only two examples of routines you may have for your family. You may have a week-end routine where everyone sleeps in until after 7 am. (Well, to be honest, I added that one in as it sounds like heaven to me at the moment!) Or you may have a weekend routine where you go to the market to buy the fruit and vegetables for the week, or where you spend family time in the garden.

Whatever additional routines you have, make sure you have weekday morning and evening routines for the kids. It is at these busiest times of the day—the peak-hour periods of morning and evening—that you want your children to be able to operate with minimal direction and complete their chores as needed so they can move on to the next stage of their day or night. As with all aspects of parenting, though, common sense and flexibility are required when following routines. For example, if our preschooler has slept in after a late night, expecting him to complete all of his usual morning chores would be unreasonable. These instances, however, are the exception and not the rule, and routines can become a natural part of daily life for kids.

Morning routines

While getting organised and introducing routines may seem like a bit of work, the benefits of taking the time to do so are enormous as routines really do help manage the first rush hour of the day. A calm and happy start to the day is not only beneficial for the kids; it can set the tone for the adults' day too.

Lay out your work clothes and child's clothes the night prior and pack a bag for childcare [to] leave at the door ready to go.

Kyrstie Barcak, mum of two

Table 1.1 shows the morning routine my kinder and school-aged kids follow during the school term.

The younger children need a visual routine, which is a simple chart with pictures showing the order in which they should complete tasks when getting ready in the morning.

Table 1.1: school morning routine

Time	Task
6.00 am onwards	Breakfast
7.00 am	Breakfast table duties
7.30 am	Brush teeth; get dressed; apply sunscreen; tidy rooms
7.50 am	Pack bags
8.10 am	Leave house

Now, as fabulous as it would be if the kids looked at their routines and worked their way independently through them, this is not how it works in reality. However, with age they've become more practised at their routines and are able to complete tasks independently. There are still times when I need to provide guidance to ensure the kids get organised in the morning, but I'm not constantly having to nag at them as they know what they should be doing.

Getting kids organised in the morning

Preparing clothes

It's much less stressful to choose clothes for toddlers and preschoolers (in particular those who like to have a say in what they're wearing) the night before. My current preschooler has a couple of favourite T-shirts that are in constant rotation. Making sure they're available the night before, when there's no hurry to be out the door, makes choosing clothes much easier. Once the clothes have been selected they can be laid out and, if they're able, preschoolers can dress themselves in the morning just like their school-aged siblings.

Getting kids organised in the morning (*cont'd*)

I encourage the older children to be responsible for organising their own clothes. My husband and I currently do the laundry, but the older children put away their own clothes, so they *should* know exactly where they are (note the emphasis on should!). It still works best to have lower primary school children lay out their clothes the night before in readiness for the next day. Allowing upper primary school children to make their own choices about organising their clothes works well as it gives them a level of autonomy over their morning routines.

Key time markers

In the mornings we have key time markers. Time markers assist children in getting themselves ready and reduce the nagging that can take place at this time of the day. We have two key times on school mornings:

⇨ 7.30 am: children have to have brushed their teeth and started getting dressed

⇨ 8.00 am: we aim to leave the house at 8.10 am, so everyone should be almost ready.

School children—who can operate more independently—may just need a reminder about the time, but for the younger children a visual morning routine helps them work through the necessary steps.

School bags

Packing their own bags is an important task for building independence in preschool and school-aged children (and decreasing the workload of parents). Again, visual charts help to ensure that children have everything they need for their school day. For example, on days when they have library, they need to have their library bag and book; on sports days they need to take their runners to school.

Keep calm

This is probably the hardest one of these tips to consider some days! I find if I try to deal calmly with situations as they arise (rather than ranting and raving at the kids), there's much less chance of an issue escalating or snowballing into a larger tantrum or drama. From practical experience, I can highlight the benefits of staying calm. There will always be the occasional morning where the preschooler finds something else—such as playing with his toys—far more appealing than getting dressed. The way I approach this can determine how big the issue becomes. I can be:

▷ *frustrated*. I can tell him angrily to get ready, while moving the toys away from him. The preschooler then has a meltdown, and becomes even more uncooperative and unwilling to get himself dressed. This loud protest lasts for a considerable period of time, raising the stress levels of everyone in the house and putting pressure on us leaving the house on time.

▷ *calm*. This approach takes slightly longer, but it's worth the effort. I help the preschooler set aside what he's playing with, so he can come back to it later, and then help him get dressed. We may take turns at putting on his clothing: he does his underpants, I do his singlet, and so on. He may not be happy with having to stop playing, but we've avoided a complete tantrum.

Mornings can be a very busy time for families, and if parents have to direct all of their children's actions, this time of the day can quickly turn into a nagging session. By creating known and age-appropriate routines for the kids, you allow them to take on greater responsibility for getting themselves ready and, best of all, the parents don't have to nag so much.

Evening routines

When our eldest child was still a preschooler, we had the same evening routine every weekday as there weren't any after-school activities to worry about. How all that's changed now we have three children at school! Depending on your family's commitments, the second rush hour can begin as soon as the kids get home from school: homework to be completed, listening to reading, driving to and from after-school activities and trying to cook dinner while consoling an overtired toddler is a very common scenario at our house.

Our after-school routine varies greatly from one day to the next. However, one thing that doesn't change is having an early evening meal—dinner now just fits within a larger window than before we had kids at school.

Before children there are certain things you can't ever imagine yourself doing, and for me one of those was eating dinner at 5.30 pm. I had heard of people doing this and wholeheartedly scoffed at the idea. To me, 5.30 pm was still part of the day! Then, suddenly, I was home all day with two children, and on some days 5.30 pm seemed like midnight.

When walking home from school in the afternoon I cut up beautiful apples for my children, which we eat as we walk. When we arrive home the children don't go to the pantry raiding the biscuits and bread as they are no longer starving and then they eat their dinner.

Georgina Rechner, mum of three

It didn't take me long to work out the reasons for and benefits of eating dinner at 5.30 pm with the kids.

- Kids are actually hungry at this time.

- Kids eat better when they're not overtired, and tiredness really starts to kick in for babies, toddlers and preschoolers after this time.

- With this tiredness comes a significant drop in kids' attention spans and their ability to sit still at the table, making mealtimes less enjoyable.

- Meals are a social time for kids too. Actually sitting down and eating a meal with them is a wonderful chance to connect and talk about their day.

Having an evening routine is also one of the best ways of getting children into bed at a reasonable time with a minimum of fuss, which increases family harmony: if kids sleep well, they're more likely to eat well; if kids are well rested and eat well, they're more likely to behave considerately and cooperatively.

At bedtime, the routine is important (dinner, wash, bed, books). What time these happen and how long they take is less important. The concept of time, which is abstract, is not relevant to kids until they are 8+ but the sequence of events is learnt early.

Julie Holden, mum of two

While our evening routine won't suit all families (because everyone has different after-school and work commitments), table 1.2 (overleaf) is included as an example of the way an evening routine can work. This was our routine when our youngest child was still a baby.

Table 1.2: evening routine

Time	Activity
5.30 pm	Dinner
6.00 pm	Bath and showers
6.20 pm	Put on pyjamas
	Take care of dirty washing; clean up bathroom; tidy up (general)
6.30 pm	Younger children (six and four years old): technology/TV time
	Older children (11 and nine years old): reading and homework
	Baby: breastfeeding (if nine year old has finished homework, then I read his story as I feed the baby)
7.00 pm	Baby goes to sleep
	Younger children: brush teeth, toilet, story and song
	Older children: technology time
7.30 pm	Younger children go to bed
	Older children: technology/TV time
8.00 pm	Nine year old: brush teeth, toilet, story, bed
	11 year old: additional technology time
8.30 pm	11 year old: brush teeth, toilet, bed

Getting kids into bed calmly

⤷ *Aim for consistent times.* Starting the bedtime routine at a similar time each night means the kids get to know when they're expected to be in bed. This familiarity makes bedtime easier to manage as children don't have an expectation that they can stay up until they feel like going to bed.

▷ *Have winding-down signals.* The steps in a bedtime routine act as signals to the kids that it's time to slow down and prepare for going to bed. Repeating the same steps each night is important so the kids can tune in to the signals. It's difficult to get children to fall asleep instantly without any time to wind down and relax.

▷ *Read a story.* I've found this to be a very enjoyable part of the bedtime routine for our family. Days can be very busy and it's easy for them to pass by without making time to read a story. Having this as part of our bedtime routine ensures we do read a story together every day and gives the kids a chance to relax before going to sleep.

▷ *Create a calm atmosphere.* When the bedtime routine begins, it's a good idea to turn off distractions such as the TV, computers and loud music. This brings a level of quiet to the house, which is calming for young children.

▷ *Prepare the bedrooms.* Plan for bedrooms to be tidy before story time. This is not the time to start tidying bedrooms or making beds; this is the final wind-down stage of the day, so don't create a whirlwind of activity.

Working parents can record talking books or videos for children so they can still be part of the bedtime routine.

Julie Holden, mum of two

Slotting cleaning into your routine

I'll be completely honest and say that cleaning is my least favourite aspect of daily life. People often think that as I'm slightly planning obsessed I must have the 'perfect' house, but I'm always happy to dispel this myth! My house is generally well organised, but with five children it meets that 'perfect' status only on very rare occasions, and even then only after a tremendous amount of work.

Rather than aspire to perfection, therefore, I've instead found a base level of cleanliness and tidiness that I need to operate from. This was an important discovery for me, not just because it mattered to me what the house looked like, but also for controlling my stress levels! Over the years I've worked out that when the piles of papers start to build up, the toilets need cleaning (very regularly with lots of boys in the house) and the floors need a vacuum and mop, my underlying stress levels increase. From this elevated baseline of stress, I found my patience was shorter, I would find more faults in what my very patient husband was doing and all I could see was mess everywhere I looked.

Every morsel that passes my children's lips MUST be consumed at the table. Otherwise I spend my day sweeping or cursing the amount of crumbs and food rubbish littered throughout the house. We always have a face washer sitting on the kitchen sink to wipe the children's hands and mouth.

Katie McIntosh, mum of eight

This scenario would inevitably end with my having a massive rant about the filthiness of the house and how I was tired of cleaning all the time (and so on and so on) — a scenario that's probably very familiar to most mothers. I realised there are key household chores that, when under control, I can turn a blind eye to (such as bookshelves that need dusting or a dirty oven).

A key task guide

One of my biggest discoveries as a stay-at-home mum was that not only do kids function better with routines, but so do parents. Daily life can be so busy it can be overwhelming at times. A common reaction to feeling overwhelmed is paralysis: doing nothing because you don't know where to start.

Whenever I was overwhelmed by the amount of cleaning needing to be done, it showed in a couple of very obvious ways. I would walk from room to room, picking up stuff here and there with no real purpose; or I would start a job only to be distracted midway by something as simple as the books on the bookshelf needing to be straightened. To remedy this situation I created a basic cleaning routine. The routine outlines the first tasks I should work on each morning after the school drop-off. Once I get going, I quickly find my rhythm and make my way through the house, but having a starter task has proved invaluable. Table 1.3 shows exactly what I mean.

Table 1.3: key task guide

Monday	Tuesday	Wednesday	Thursday	Friday
Cook evening meal	Toilets and basins	Cook evening meal	Laundry	Toilets and basins
Benches	Laundry	Vacuum	Benches	Vacuum
Vacuum				

This routine lets me switch to autopilot. I can come in from the school run each weekday morning and know which task to tackle straight away. For example, if we have swimming lessons after school on Mondays, I know my key task on Monday morning is to prepare the evening meal. Having it prepared early helps make the after-school rush much more manageable. If our preschooler and toddler are not able to amuse themselves and need my attention I put the other key tasks for the day on hold and play with the kids. I then try to find other blocks of time during the day to complete them. Just after lunch when the kids have been refuelled is often a good time for catching up on unfinished tasks.

The key tasks are my priority prompts — they keep me on track. However, they're not all of my day's tasks. There are days when I don't follow this routine at all as we may have appointments, play dates or other higher priority tasks. However, the guide is imprinted in my head and if there aren't any other commitments, I can move straight on to purposeful work without having to think about it.

The 15-minute block

Prior to having children, I used to love the feeling of sitting on the couch and looking around the house knowing that *everything* had just been cleaned. I still remember that lovely feeling, but after my second child was born I finally gave up the idea of trying to clean the entire house in one day. With feeding, playing and napping to juggle the cleaning around, it simply wasn't a realistic objective.

When I had only two children I worked on a system where I'd break down the house cleaning into rooms. I'd complete one room at a time and make my way through all of the rooms in the house over one week. Then along came baby number three, baby number four and baby number five! It was after our last child was born that I had another realisation — my objective of cleaning whole rooms at a time might work occasionally (depending on the sleeping pattern of the baby and the mood of the preschooler), but it wasn't a routine I could depend upon to successfully clean the house.

Thankfully, at this time I also came across the very practical concept of working in 15-minute blocks. It wouldn't be going too far to say that this revolutionised my approach to cleaning and, more importantly, gave me the feeling I was staying on top of things. I highlighted my key tasks in table 1.3 and you can see that—with the exception of cooking the family meal—all of these tasks can be completed in 15-minute blocks. This works because:

- the children can easily occupy themselves for this length of time

- starting a task you know you can complete without having to stop halfway through can give you a feeling of achievement even when you feel there's just too much to cope with

- this amount of cleaning makes an instant difference to the tidiness and/or cleanliness of the house

- if you don't love cleaning (and not many of us do), it's easier to stick to a single task knowing that it will only take 15 minutes.

Once I arrive home from the school drop-off, I start my first 15-minute block for the day (apart from the days when cooking is my first key task, in which case I begin with that even if it takes longer than 15 minutes). I set my toddler and preschooler up with an activity and then hop straight into it. If I've completed one 15-minute block and the children are still happily playing, I move swiftly on to another one.

Look at your daily routine and find places where you can slot in 15-minute cleaning blocks. The more house cleaning becomes part of your daily routine, the more likely you are to get it done. Fifteen-minute blocks work best when you can fit them around constant events in your day such as:

- before leaving to take the kids to school
- after school drop-off in the morning
- before putting your toddler to bed
- before school pick-up in the afternoon
- while the kids are having afternoon tea.

There are numerous cleaning activities that can be completed in 15 minutes. Here's a list to get you started:

- picking up and packing away anything that's not in its place
- cleaning toilets
- wiping bathroom benches, basins and mirrors
- wiping down kitchen cupboards
- dusting one room
- vacuuming the main living areas
- putting on, hanging out, folding a load of washing
- emptying and cleaning bins
- changing bed linen
- cleaning the windows in one room.

Involving the family

Although I'm the primary cleaner in our house, this doesn't mean I should be responsible for everything! As part of our family's weekly routines I've made sure there are plenty of opportunities for my kids and husband to contribute to the upkeep of our family home.

Getting the kids to help

It's important that children don't think a 'clean-up fairy' lives in their house. If you continually remove the rubbish from their bedrooms or take the dirty clothes to the laundry for them, kids won't learn how much work these jobs involve. By delegating some responsibility to each child, not only will you make them aware of the work involved in keeping the household running smoothly, but they will also learn valuable independence and life skills.

For me, this means that sometimes I have to live with some mess and untidiness until the kids get home from school and clean up after themselves. This can be hard to do when you have to walk past their bedrooms a number of times a day and see the mess scattered all over the floor, so now I close the doors until the kids are home.

Starting kids off early with age-appropriate jobs is the best way to get them involved with the cleaning and daily household chores. Table 1.4 (overleaf) is an example of age-appropriate tasks. Note that it assumes an add-on approach where, for example, 11 year olds would be doing some of the tasks from each age group below them as well as the tasks appropriate for their age.

Getting your partner to help

I'm fortunate to have a husband who helps keep the house clean and tidy. This, however, wasn't always the case, and it's been a transitional change. I found the way to reach an agreement with my husband where he would contribute more to the household upkeep was to:

- discuss my expectations and needs with him
- allocate him set tasks (anyone can work well with a routine!)

- realise that he doesn't see what I see. So, if a job needs doing, I have to ask him to do it rather than martyr myself by doing it in a huff!

- give him space to complete a task and accept that he may not do it the way I do (I still find this a bit hard, but I'm working on it!)

- teach him about 15-minute blocks.

Table 1.4: children's age-appropriate tasks

Age	Tasks
2–3 year olds The aim is not for perfection, but for children to begin learning to do things for themselves and to contribute to the running of the family home. They will need assistance.	✶ Take breakfast dishes away from table. ✶ Make bed and tidy room. ✶ Wipe and sweep up own messes throughout the day. ✶ Pack away toys and generally tidy up. ✶ Take condiments to table for evening meal. ✶ Take own plate away from dinner table. ✶ Place dirty clothes in laundry basket. ✶ Return towel to bathroom.
4–5 year olds The aim is for children to know their own job routines and to carry them out without having to be reminded. They may still need some assistance.	✶ Return cereal boxes to cupboard after breakfast. ✶ Pack kinder bag or school bag. ✶ Unpack kinder bag or school bag and hand over any notices. ✶ Set place mats for dinner. ✶ As required, help match up socks when laundry is being folded. ✶ Assist in the garden with sweeping and raking.

Age	Tasks
6–7 year olds The aim is for children to now be completing their tasks independently.	* Place milk and juice back in the fridge after breakfast. * Empty rubbish bins. * Set cutlery for dinner. * Put own laundered clothes away. * On weekends, help make morning and afternoon tea. * Cook treats such as scones and muffins. * Help sort laundry into colour groupings.
8–10 year olds The aim is for children to be taking on tasks that require more time, and to complete a household task rather than only a part of it.	* Stack dishwasher. * Empty compost bin and clean container. * Make drinks for evening meal. * Vacuum own bedroom. * Help cook a family meal as required. * Assist with folding clean laundry. * Help with weeding the garden.
11–12 year olds The aim is to have a variety of indoor and outdoor jobs for children of this age.	* Unstack dishwasher. * Vacuum whole house as required. * Regularly cook a family meal by themselves. * Mow lawn. * Hang out washing. * Put away groceries.

It's important that the job of cleaning the family home isn't left to any one individual. Take time to divide up the workload and include house cleaning as part of your family's daily routines. Giving every family member some responsibilities appropriate for their age will contribute towards keeping the house at a level of cleanliness and tidiness you can cope with.

Taming the laundry beast

There's no bigger part of daily life for a growing family than doing the laundry. As you can probably imagine, with five children we generate a significant amount of washing. Naturally, this results in a large amount of folding and ironing, and I admit to not always having it under control. After a particularly busy week, you'll see a mountain of clean washing needing attention in our front room. I still manage to get the washing done (out of necessity), but if time is tight, the folding in particular tends to be neglected. The flow-on effect of not having the washing up to date is never very pretty—'Mum, where are my footy shorts?'; 'Mum, where are my school socks?')—so the incentive to keep it in check is considerable.

After number eight I gave up ironing. I have a fantastic washing machine and dryer. I now hang very little on the clothes line. I realise this is environmentally irresponsible but it's great for my sanity and the washing turnover.

Katie McIntosh, mum of eight

In table 1.3, you'll see I've included laundry on Tuesdays and Thursdays. Like most mums with a large family, I usually do the washing every day, but these are the two days when I *have to* make sure I do a load of washing. The school children have two sets of school uniforms and one sports uniform each. They all have sport on Thursdays, so from their school schedule I know that for them to have clean uniforms I must wash on Tuesdays and Thursdays. It's been helpful to note this, so when we have super busy days and are out and about a lot, I know on which days I need to do a load of washing.

I like to determine my minimum requirements so I can adequately plan my week to fit them in. This can be just a mental note allowing me to operate on autopilot. Being able to function on autopilot can be incredibly important when you have young children, particularly when you're overly sleep-deprived or coping with several sick kids. It means you can still meet your minimum requirements (in this case having clean clothes) to keep daily life humming along without having to spend time working out what it is you have to get done.

Keeping the laundry tasks under control

Here is a collection of my tips and also tips from other mothers who kindly shared them with me on my blog. Not all of them will suit your family, but there are fantastic strategies listed here that will allow you to tame the beast that is the family laundry pile.

▷ Avoid letting it build up. Aim for daily loads as it's always worse when you are knee-deep in dirty clothes.

▷ If you have a timer function on your washing machine, load the machine up the night before and set the timer so the washing is ready when you come home from the school run.

▷ Hang more delicate clothes such as business shirts on hangers and fold the rest of the clothes as neatly as possible in a basket to reduce the amount of ironing.

Deb Hodgkin, mum of two <www.science-at-home.org>

Keeping the laundry tasks under control (*cont'd*)

▷ When hanging the washing on the line, do it with types of clothes grouped together and socks in pairs, as this makes the folding task much easier.
Claire Lane, stepmum of two <www.urbanassistant.com.au>

▷ Aim to fold clothes that don't need ironing as soon as you take them off the clothes horse or clothes line rather than putting them back in a basket.

▷ When buying socks for the kids, think about buying mostly the same type and colour of socks — it makes pairing them up so much easier.
Fleur Morgan-Payler, mum of two

▷ Involve the kids and your partner in sharing the workload.

When I started working full time at the beginning of this year, I made myself go out and buy extra pairs of pants, shirts and jumpers for my son, because I knew I wouldn't be able to keep up with washing every other day as the single mum of a toddler. I just wasn't able to keep on top of things when working full time.

Jasmine Norris, mum of one

Holding family meetings

We've been using family meetings as a tool for managing and planning our life for more than eight years now. For our family, the aim of family meetings is to:

• provide an organised way of dealing with contentious issues

• create a forum where all voices are equal

- create a space where we can jointly plan fun activities and other parts of home life

- role model and offer opportunities for the kids to practise decision making, negotiation and problem-solving skills

- create a sense of ownership of family decisions.

During the meetings we try to encourage the kids to take part in solving problems and generating ideas. If a child has an issue they want raised at the family meeting, they have to bring along a solution and not just the problem.

We started having family meetings when our eldest child was four and our second child was two. When you only have children of this age at a family meeting, it can feel slightly strange! However, starting the meetings with kids at this age means they'll grow up accepting them as part of their life: they'll expect to have meetings regularly, and will be prepared to contribute their thoughts and opinions.

Guidelines for family meetings

We developed guidelines so everyone would understand how family meetings were to be run. Depending on the age of your kids and your family dynamics, our guidelines may not necessarily be a perfect match, but you can use the key headings that follow to develop your own guidelines for providing a strong framework for your family meetings.

Set a time and frequency

Set a regular time and day when everyone is most likely to be at home. Decide how often you want to meet. (We currently meet fortnightly.)

Choose a suitable place

The meetings need to be held in a place that's free from distractions. (We use the dinner table.)

Decide who should attend

All family members over the age of two are expected to attend our meetings.

Rotate the convenor or chair

At our place we take it in turns to convene meetings so that everyone has a go. Mum or Dad assists the toddler and preschooler until they get the hang of things.

Take minutes

We take minutes at each meeting and these are always reviewed as the first agenda item at the next family meeting. The children who can write also have a turn at taking the minutes.

Choose a time frame

Due to the age of the children attending, we aim to make our meetings last no longer than 20 minutes.

Raise hands

Everyone must raise their hand and be acknowledged by the convenor before they may speak. This practice teaches children that in meetings not only do you have an opportunity to talk, but you also need to listen to others.

Follow agenda items

Although we use a formal structure for our family meetings, they're generally lighthearted and fun. Quite often the meeting is more of a sharing time, where kids or adults provide updates to the family on areas of their life or items of interest.

Ensure agreement

We keep working on a resolution for each matter raised until we have one that all family members can agree on. This is critical to the success of our family meetings. No-one should leave the family meeting feeling they haven't been listened to or their needs haven't been taken into consideration.

The benefits of family meetings

Our regular family meetings have allowed us to establish a forum for resolving problems and sharing ideas. When a contentious issue arises in the middle of a busy day it can be very helpful if I can assure everyone I'm putting the matter on the agenda for the next meeting. It instantly takes the heat out of the situation and makes the kids start thinking about solutions.

Family meetings allow for all family members to feel their contribution has been taken into account, regardless of their age. This doesn't mean the kids get exactly what they want, but it teaches them about compromise and that sometimes getting agreement means making concessions. It also teaches the older children to work out what are the 'must-haves' in relation to their issues, and makes them practise using persuasive arguments to attain what they want. Most importantly, as the kids have had an input regarding the decisions being made at family meetings, there's a much better chance they'll stick to those decisions in the future.

Taking action

- Establish morning and evening routines for your children.

- Determine your base operating level of cleanliness and tidiness for the family home.

- Create a key task guide that will help you maintain this base level.

- Complete your key tasks using 15-minute blocks of activity.

- Allocate household chores to every member of the family as part of their daily routines.

- Determine your minimum requirements for laundry across the week and incorporate them into your key task guide.

- Use family meetings as a tool for managing and planning daily family life.

Chapter 2

Meals

Meals play a large part in family life. As parents, we have to think about what to feed the kids and when; we have to buy and prepare the food; and then we have to try to get the kids to eat what we've cooked! This aspect of daily life can take up significant amounts of time and can also cause considerable stress. But it doesn't necessarily have to be that way. One of my biggest realisations as a parent has been that it's worth the effort of taking time to plan meals. It has reduced the amount of time I spend on meals and has helped make mealtimes a more enjoyable part of the day.

Menu planning

Menu planning helps solve the dreaded question that arises at about 4 or 5 pm every day: 'What's for dinner?' Before having kids, I would rarely give a thought to dinner until I arrived home from work. I would even make a quick trip to the supermarket to buy additional ingredients if I felt like having something special.

With several children, there's no such thing as a quick trip to the supermarket. Nor is it always an easy job to cook with small children hanging off your hips and legs. As I mentioned at the start of the book, menu planning was one of the first projects I set myself when I decided to take a more prepared approach to organisation at home. It's the best way to streamline a very repetitive task and create order during a busy part of the day.

To give me a few moments [of] peace while I make dinner, I get out a large plastic bowl with water and a squeeze of dishwashing liquid. My toddler loves to stir with a whisk to make bubbles. I just use a little water so it is not too messy and put it all down on a tea towel and it keeps her happily occupied.

Christie Burnett, mum of one
<www.childhood101.com>

Family menu plans can be as brief or as detailed as you like. A menu plan covers every day of the week and all the meals you intend to cook for the family. If you're very eager, you can plan breakfast, lunch, dinner and snacks for the whole day. I've never found the need to go this far, so I just document what our evening meals will be each day of the week. Once I've chosen our meals I can easily prepare a shopping list to make sure I'll have all the required ingredients on hand.

I plan the meals at the start of the week on the whiteboard on the fridge so what I want is defrosted by the time I get home from work. I cook a double lot of things like a casserole or spaghetti sauce using the slow cooker, then freeze half in small portions (quicker to defrost or just defrost as much as you need and fit[s] in the freezer better).

Marita Shepherd, mum of two

Why menu planning works

In essence, menu planning works because it saves you time. As with a lot of other tasks, the thought of sitting down and planning is actually worse than the deed itself. Once you get going you can quickly choose meals for your family. It actually takes a lot less time than if I were to consider the question, 'What will we have for dinner?' every single day.

Menu planning is another system that allows you to run on autopilot in the middle of busy days with the kids or at work. The hard work of thinking about what to cook has been done, so in the lead-up to mealtime it's just a matter of referring to the meal plan and then cooking. The additional bonus of menu planning is it also helps with other areas of daily life.

- *It saves money.* By planning the meals for the week you can purchase all the ingredients you need at one time. No more rushed trips, where you end up buying much more than intended. Planning allows you to take advantage of supermarket specials by selecting meals that use ingredients which are on sale.

- *It supports healthy eating.* As you have the ingredients on hand and have already thought about what to cook, you're much less likely to substitute your planned meal for takeaway or a less healthy home-cooked option (like toast!).

- *It decreases stress levels.* The late afternoon and early evening time with small children can be fraught with overtiredness, tears and whining. To then have to think of what to cook and perhaps even have to leave the house to purchase ingredients can really increase stress levels. Menu planning eliminates this source of stress from the equation.

- *It supports regular eating as a family.* If meal planning is left to the last minute, it can be very tempting to whip something up quickly for the kids and then have to organise a separate meal later for the adults. By having planned what to cook, you're much more likely to sit and eat with the kids.

- *It offers variety.* Planning your family's weekly meals means you can ensure efficient use of food yet still keep variety by using the same ingredients in different combinations.

An instant guide to menu planning

I've been menu planning regularly for about eight years and I've finetuned the process I use. I now menu plan on a monthly basis, but the process can be applied to any time frame. These are the steps I follow.

Step 1: decide on a daily theme

Choose a style or category of meal for each day of the week. This makes planning for periods longer than a week much easier and quicker. My standard categories are:

- pasta-based dishes

- meals with rice

- slow-cooker meals

- bulk meals (I use the leftovers from these for other meals)

- quick meals (up to 15 minutes of preparation)

- meals that my husband and the kids can cook

- meat and vegetables

- soups

- vegetarian.

We have a number of easy and quick meals that we do on the nights that I have been working, such as tacos or tuna mornay, so that the kids don't have too long to wait between getting home and eating. I decide what meal we will be having the night before so that I can make sure I defrost the meat or buy any ingredients that we may need.

Leona Campitelli, mum of three

Once I've taken into account after-school activities, weather and weekend commitments, I allocate each of the categories to a day of the week.

- *Monday:* pasta-based dish (gymnastics from 4 pm to 5 pm)

- *Tuesday:* slow-cooker meal—cooking can be done earlier in the day (swimming from 5.30 pm to 6.00 pm)

- *Wednesday:* meal with rice (football training from 5.30 pm to 6.45 pm)

- *Thursday:* bulk meal (often by Friday I really don't feel like cooking so a bulk meal on Thursday is good preparation)

- *Friday:* leftovers (football training from 4.30 pm to 5.30 pm)

- *Saturday:* meals that my husband or the kids can cook

- *Sunday:* meat and vegetables (football at 8.45 am and 11.00 am).

Step 2: consider seasons and specials

Fresh fruit and vegetables are always much tastier and cheaper when they're in season. I find out which fruits and vegetables are in season and take this into consideration when selecting meals. I also use the supermarket catalogues for inspiration, checking out which key ingredients are on special and selecting meals that use them for our menu plan. I note these down to start the list of meals that I'll choose from.

Step 3: get input from the family

My kids are quite used to my menu planning. When I have a monthly menu-planning session, I ask them to suggest up to four meals they'd like included.

There are three key benefits to involving the kids.

- They're happier to eat the meals as they know their favourite meal is coming up too.

- It provides opportunities to talk about seasonal food; for example, why we don't often eat casseroles in summer and which vegetables are in season.

- It means I have to choose fewer meals myself!

I also hunt down my husband to see whether he has any requests for our evening meals. I write everyone's suggestions on my growing meal list.

Step 4: allocate the meals

Now I have a comprehensive list of meals to choose from. I use a monthly template to slot meals against the relevant days so they fit into the daily categories I've selected. As mentioned earlier, you can plan for any time frame; however, I've found monthly to be the optimal period for our family. Having done this so many times now, I can plan our meals for the month in 35 minutes. The end result can be seen in table 2.1. You can download a monthly menu planning template at <www.planningwithkids.com/resources>.

Table 2.1: monthly menu planner

Week beginning	Monday: Pasta	Tuesday: Slow cooker	Wednesday: Meal with rice	Thursday: Bulk meal	Friday: Leftovers	Saturday: Kids or Dad	Sunday: Meat and veggies
2 August	Penne bake	Chicken noodle soup	Beef stir fry	Mexibake	Leftovers	Chicken wings and baked potatoes	Roast lamb and veggies
9 August	Pasta with chicken and spinach	Beef stroganoff	Tuna rice	Chicken schnitzel and steamed veggies	Leftovers	Souvlaki	Chicken schnitzel and steamed veggies
16 August	Spaghetti bolognaise	Pumpkin soup	Moroccan minted beef	Shepherd's pie	Leftovers	Tacos	Roast beef and veggies
23 August	Pasta carbonara	Beef curry	Spicy chutney chicken	Pasties	Leftovers	Fried rice	Sausage and veggies

Shopping for growing families

Once I've created a menu plan, not only has this made mealtime easier, but the task of shopping for groceries has now been simplified too. The menu plan allows me to easily collate a shopping list to take to the supermarket.

Shopping lists

Shopping lists are the key to efficient shopping for our family. I have two options for creating a shopping list: I can manually scan the meals I've chosen into the menu plan and write up a list; or, I can use a free menu planner tool such as the one provided on the blog. Go to <www.planningwithkids.com/menuplanner/index.php>. This menu planner has a simple, five-step procedure:

1   Select the date for the beginning of the week.

2   Choose your meals.

3   Choose the number of serves required for each meal.

4   Tick the boxes of the recipes you wish to print out.

5   Print out the menu plan, recipes and shopping list.

The shopping list is arranged by food type, making the task of finding the items you need when you're at the supermarket quicker and easier. As the menu planner only looks at the evening meals, our shopping list is still a work in progress and needs to have other groceries and household items added to it. To help build a comprehensive shopping list that ensures no last-minute rushed trips to the supermarket, there are a couple of other lists I refer to:

• *Pantry checklists.* I have checklists stuck to the inside of the pantry cupboards. As I run out of items or items are close to running out, I place a tick next to them on the checklists. When it comes time to write my shopping list, I simply add the ticked items to it.

- *Lunchbox items.* Fresh fruit and vegetables are the easiest way to fill the kids' lunchboxes. To retain some variety, I refer to lists of seasonal fruit and vegetables that I know the kids will eat.

Where to shop

Living in a capital city, I'm lucky to have several options when it comes to shopping for our family groceries. My shopping routine over the past few years has consisted of a monthly online grocery shop, a monthly visit to the butcher and a weekly trip to a fresh fruit and vegetable market. Not all of these may be available where you live, but it's worth considering them if they are.

Online shopping

The first time I shopped online it took me ages, and I thought it was a very time-consuming process. However, it's really only slow the first couple of times you do it—after that it's a super-efficient way to shop because:

- all your previous orders are listed and you can quickly tick the items you wish to add to your trolley the next time you shop

- you can buy in bulk because the goods are delivered to your door

- you can see exactly how much you're spending and either remove or add discretionary items so you stay within your budget

- you can easily compare prices as products can be listed by unit price

- you can do it on your own!

Markets

We shop weekly at a nearby market, and have found that buying fruit and vegetables at markets is significantly cheaper than purchasing them from the supermarket. In addition, the quality is far superior. If you haven't tried a market, consider these tips for your first visit.

- Take with you a list of prices for the items you buy regularly from the supermarket so you can compare.

- Allow yourself plenty of time to walk around the market first to note the varying prices and quality of the produce. Even at markets you'll find stallholders who don't offer value for money.

- Go back and make your purchases, noting how much you pay and the location of the stall that you bought them from. If you know the location of the stalls you like, this will make the process quicker next time.

- When you get home, do some quick calculations to see how much you saved. It can be more of an effort to go to a market than to the local shops, so having a concrete dollar amount can be a great incentive to keep up the habit. Table 2.2 illustrates how much you could save on your grocery bill by going to the market.

This is just a sample of the savings we made on five of about 15 items. Even if you deduct the extra petrol it costs us (about $3.00) to drive to the market, we still save significantly.

Table 2.2: market savings

	Supermarket	Market	Quantity	Saving
Red capsicums (kg)	$6.99	$3.99	1.5	$4.50
Apples (kg)	$4.98	$2.50	5	$12.40
Carrots (kg)	$2.29	$1.49	2.5	$2.00
Pumpkin (whole)	$2.99	$2.00	2	$1.98
Lettuce (iceberg)	$2.99	$1.99	1	$1.00
Total				**$21.88**

Butcher

For a number of years I worked on the false assumption that because supermarkets have chains they should be able to deliver cheaper prices on meat. I was very much mistaken. Meat is often very expensive at the main supermarkets in Australia. From my experience, I've also found the quality of meat superior at a local butcher shop. Not all butchers are cheap, so I spent some time comparing prices and quality and have found a local butcher shop that provides great meat at a great price. When looking for a local butcher, think about whether:

- they offer discounts for bulk purchases. For example, chicken breasts are $3.00 per kilogram cheaper if I buy more than 2 kilograms at a time

- you can ring in your order and pick it up later — a great convenience when you're shopping with little ones

- they have regular specials you can take advantage of (not all of them do)

- there's a market near you that sells meat. Big markets such as the Queen Victoria Market in Melbourne — and (increasingly) farmers markets throughout the country — are selling local meat at great prices.

Discount retailers and warehouse clubs

In recent years, Australia has seen the introduction of a number of international stores such as Aldi and Costco. They can help you save significant amounts of money, but you should keep the following in mind:

- *Buy only what you need.* Cheap is tempting, but remember to stick to your list.

- *Buy in bulk.* I love buying items in bulk as this offers great value (when I know we'll use everything). To make the most of bulk buying, consider teaming up with a friend and sharing the goods if the discounts only apply for large volumes.

- *Be prepared to try new brands.* Don't expect to see all your familiar brands at these stores. I've tried different brands for products such as tomato paste, pasta sauces, plastic wrap, chocolate and nappies and have found the quality comparable.

- *Factor in the extra fees.* Some of these stores have surcharges for credit cards. There can also be costs for purchasing bags, as well as membership and parking fees that you might have avoided elsewhere.

- *Add up the transport costs.* Did you have to pay tolls to get there, and how much petrol did it cost?

Enjoying your mealtimes

With our meals selected and ingredients bought, we're halfway towards enjoying a family meal. *Most* evenings (life is never perfect!) we sit down together to eat our dinner and enjoy each other's company. As we eat early in the evening from Monday to Friday, only I eat with the kids. Then, on the weekends, my husband is around to eat with us.

Here are some tips on how to make mealtimes more enjoyable for everyone, based on my past experience.

Involve the kids in menu planning

Allowing the kids to help me with menu planning makes them feel included, so they're happier to eat whatever I serve.

Have a set time range for evening meals

It's easy for my toddler and preschooler to be past their hungry time and not eat a proper meal because it's too late. Having an early time range (ours is from 5.00 pm to 5.30 pm) means the younger children will actually eat their dinner more often.

Eat at the table

I find it's much easier to get my children to focus on their meal if they're sitting up at a table. It's less tempting for small children to wander off and play with toys mid meal, and it also provides the best scenario for teaching children the social etiquette of eating a meal with others.

Get the children to help you

It's important for children to understand the work that goes into preparing the family meal. If they each have a small job to do, they become more involved and aware of the process.

Serve age-appropriate portions

About eleven years ago I went to a parenting seminar on eating and toilet training for toddlers, run by Tweddle Child and Family

Enjoying your mealtimes (*cont'd*)

Health Services. They suggested when you serve up meals for a toddler, halve what you originally put on their plate and then halve it again. This is more likely to be an age-appropriate serve for a toddler. This was fantastic advice and has worked well for us. Toddlers who are hungry will ask for more, but they can be overwhelmed by large amounts of food on their plate. It also makes me feel better when I see an empty bowl.

Turn off distractions

I love having music on around the house, but even that must go off at mealtimes as it can easily distract the children. I also let any phonecalls go through to message bank so I'm not distracted by leaving the table. On occasion, when I'm tempted to answer a call, I always end up regretting it. The younger kids lose focus on the meal and it's impossible to get them to regain it.

Model appropriate behaviour

Children will follow the example set for them, so I always try to model the behaviour that I would like them to replicate. I'm not crazy about a number of vegetables, but setting the right example means eating those vegetables without complaint!

Encourage conversation

Mealtime is my greatest source of information about what's going on at school and kinder. The kids have had time to unwind and have relaxed a bit, so I find open-ended questions such as 'What did you play at lunchtime?', or 'Who did you play with at kinder?' encourage the kids to start telling me interesting stories about their day.

Remove the battlelines

Just as you can't make a baby sleep, I don't think you can make a child eat either. I've learned that getting kids to eat a meal can be a real battle. Spending time and money cooking a healthy meal only for it to be rejected and uneaten is incredibly frustrating. To make mealtimes enjoyable in our house, no-one is forced to eat their dinner; however, there's no substitute meal if they don't like what's been served: they'll have to wait until breakfast for something to eat.

Only focus on the big issues

To keep the tone of the evening meal light, I try not to comment on every single thing each child does that's not ideal. If I did, some nights that would be the only talking going on. I have core behaviours that I expect the children to meet and I monitor those, but if they accidentally slurp their spaghetti, or if the younger ones use their hands occasionally when trying to cut up their food, I let these go. Too much negativity can bring the mood down and close off conversation.

Try to teach table manners from an early age and introduce forks, spoons and knives (blunt butter knives are great) so that they are a normal part of eating.

Lou Woods, mum of four

Letting the family cook

In the monthly menu-planning template, one evening meal per week is set aside for my husband or the kids to cook. This wasn't always the case, so having a night off from cooking is a great break for me.

The change also didn't happen overnight. It evolved as my blogging workload increased and the children grew older. The benefits of giving the family a chance to do the cooking are not only mine either. My husband is now far more capable in the kitchen and has increased the selection of meals he can cook from five to about ten. My eldest son—who has begun cooking meals on his own—has more self-confidence and is building on his independence skills. To get your family involved in the kitchen with less of a fight, you should set expectations, familiarise your family with the kitchen and find child-friendly recipes.

Find 10 meals your kids love to eat and alternate serving them during the week. From six or seven years old get them to help prepare and cook dinner. A child always finishes eating something they help to make. Start a veggie or herb garden with your kids and use [the veggies and herbs] in your meals—you'd be surprised what a nine year old will eat if he's grown it himself.

Stephen Fulton, dad of three

Setting expectations

I first needed to work out what assistance I wanted with cooking the evening meals. How often did I want someone else to cook, and who did I think could do this? My husband and I discussed his involvement and we agreed on him being solely responsible for the meal on Saturdays and assisting on Sundays. Having clear expectations set up between us meant we each had our accountabilities. He was to cook the meal and I was to leave him in peace to do it, without constantly looking over his shoulder.

We then had a similar conversation with our eldest son. We had just begun teaching him to cook, so we then talked about how often he could cook a meal for the family on his own. We all agreed on once a month.

Introducing the family to the kitchen

Not everyone feels comfortable in the kitchen, but that doesn't have to be an excuse for keeping them out of it. I've witnessed how practice and familiarity can make a big difference in cooking a meal. To introduce my husband and my kids to the kitchen I've used a very similar process.

- *Health and safety lessons.* The kids are in the kitchen quite a bit with me, so it's valuable to remind them of kitchen safety and health basics such as:

  — washing hands

  — tying hair back

  — power-point and electricity safety

  — how to face pot handles

  — how to handle knives

  — cutting away from yourself.

- *Start small.* A gradual introduction is easier than jumping in the deep end. Starting the kids with small cooking projects such as scones, muffins and slices, and then progressing to light meals such as scrambled eggs, builds their confidence through success. They're then willing to try more complex recipes.

- *Watch and learn.* Just being in the kitchen and watching how things are done is really helpful. When learning how to prepare a meal, my husband prefers to watch me cook it in its entirety. He writes notes on a copy of the recipe while I'm cooking so he'll feel confident about cooking the meal by himself.

- *Doing it together.* The kids learn by watching me prepare a meal. The next time we prepare that dish the children cook it with me. This time they're in charge of the cooking and I supervise and answer any questions. This stage can take a while to perfect. For example, my eldest son only needs help once with some meals. However, for other, more complex recipes he may need me around a few times before he feels comfortable cooking it on his own.

- *Going solo.* Once they feel confident about cooking a meal, I let the kids be solely responsible for putting it together—from the first steps of finding the ingredients, to serving it and cleaning up. It can be tempting to step in and correct anything you see that might not be right. Sometimes I find it easier to walk away! I try not to intervene unless there's a safety issue involved. Kids tend to learn best from making mistakes and working things out by themselves.

Recipes for kids to cook

Table 2.3 shows some examples of recipes that my children and my 'non-cook' husband prepare for the family. All the recipes listed can be found on the blog at <www.planningwithkids.com/family-friendly-recipes>.

Family-friendly food

Not every meal I serve up for dinner is received joyfully by all my kids. Each child has their own distinct set of likes and dislikes. The kids have input to the menu plan, so their preferences are taken into account, but as the parent I also endeavour to expose them to new foods, textures and combinations. I've learned through many rejections and wasted meals that while trying to do this, I still need to keep an emphasis on making the food for our evening meals family-friendly.

Table 2.3: recipes for kids and partners to cook

Appropriate for	Recipes
3–5 year olds (with help)	✳ Scones ✳ Muffins ✳ Chocolate balls ✳ Vegemite scrolls ✳ Traffic-light sandwiches
6–9 year olds (independently after practice)	✳ Homemade pizza ✳ Homemade chips (oven baked) ✳ Scrambled eggs ✳ Egg and bacon tarts ✳ 100s of biscuits
10–12 year olds (independently after practice)	✳ Tacos ✳ Sausages and salad ✳ Tuna rice ✳ Spaghetti bolognaise ✳ Banana cake
'Non-cook' partner	✳ Beef stir-fry ✳ Fried rice ✳ Baked penne with bacon ✳ Souvlaki ✳ Chicken lasagne

Getting kids to eat

We've modified our approach to eating meals over the years. Originally, we used to offer the kids dessert after every meal and this often became a bargaining element. I remember saying things like, 'Eat three more bites, then you can have dessert', particularly if I was getting them to try something new. But as the children grew older, they'd ask, 'What's for dessert?' to find out whether it was worth eating those extra spoonfuls or not. Mealtime could become a battle over how much more was to be eaten.

To avoid this scenario, we agreed at a family meeting that we'd have dessert only twice a week, and the children would get to eat it regardless of whether they'd eaten their main meal or not. This was under the explicit understanding that once mealtime finishes there's no further option of eating food for the rest of the evening. If the children choose not to eat their meal, I don't discuss it with them other than to explain that it's their decision and that they'll have to wait until breakfast for something to eat.

There are nights when, after not eating their meal, one of the kids will say they're hungry. This comes mainly from the younger ones, as the older three don't bother telling me any more. When I respond I aim to be empathetic and calm, and I explain they can have breakfast in the morning. This doesn't always end quietly or without tears; however, it happens infrequently as the kids have now grown used to the consequences of not eating their dinner.

Meals kids love

It's possible to serve up meals that are healthy *and* that kids will love. While the kids do have different preferences, self-serve meals tend to be winners with all kids. These are the types of meals where you set food out on the table and everyone selects what they want.

We have a number of different styles of self-serve meals like this, but the format is same: a serving of meat and a selection of pre-cut vegetables and salads to choose from. I find with these meals the kids eat more fresh vegetables. They're empowered by choice and they particularly love using little serving tongs to serve themselves.

Another bonus with these types of self-serve meals is that I generally have at least one child in the kitchen helping me prepare the food: slicing cheese, peeling carrots, tearing lettuce and cutting capsicum are all tasks that can easily be done by little hands.

Some self-serve meals that my kids love are:

- tacos
- chicken schnitzel and salad
- homemade hamburgers and salad
- pan-fried fish with salad
- salad rolls
- sausages and salad
- souvlaki
- baked potatoes
- chicken wings, corn and baked potatoes.

You can find these recipes on the blog at <www. planningwithkids.com/family-friendly-recipes>. We generally have one self-serve meal a week, which is always warmly received by the kids.

School lunches

One of the highlights of school holidays for me is not having to make school lunches. I find this task one of those repetitive and boring—although essential—ones of parenting: a perfect task for which to create a process!

Creating a school lunchbox process

School mornings can be stressful if there's too much to do and too much to think about. Our school lunchbox process streamlines the workload and takes the mental energy out of thinking about what to give the kids.

- *Establish how much food you need.* Through trial and error I've worked out how much food my children need to get them through the day. My seven-year-old daughter, for example, eats much less than her 12-year-old brother, so this is one thing I consider when packing the lunchboxes.

- *Create a school lunchbox guide.* Once I know how much food is enough for each child, I build a guide to refer to when making the school lunches. Having a guide also makes it easier to delegate this task to someone else—such as my husband—as the need arises. I find that five to six items (my daughter only needs five) from a good mix of food groups such as those listed here is enough for my children:

  _ a core lunch item

  _ a whole piece of fruit

  _ veggie sticks

  _ cut fruit

  _ a home-baked treat

  _ a selection of crackers and/or dried fruit.

- *Prepare as much as you can the night before.* Much of the preparation for school lunches can be completed the night before. Table 2.4 shows some examples.

Table 2.4: night-time lunchbox preparation

Item	Task
Fruit and vegetables	Cut up fruit and vegetables and store in fridge. I find that watermelon, rockmelon, strawberries and so on can be cut the night before and placed in airtight containers until morning
Sandwiches	Cut up fresh ingredients for sandwiches if required. I like to make fresh sandwiches every day, purely as a personal preference. Some people are happy to make up large batches of sandwiches and freeze them in advance. I often grate carrot, shred lettuce, slice tomato etc. the night before so that I only have to make up the sandwich in the morning
Dry snacks	Make up cracker and dried-fruit packs and place them in lunchbox
Treats	Wrap up cake or muffins and place in lunchbox

- *Have a regular baking day/s.* I've found that having a regular baking day helps ensure there's a home-cooked treat in the children's school lunches. Throughout most of the year I have one to two baking sessions per week: one on Sunday evening (which I do quickly by myself) and another on a week day, when I bake with our toddler and preschooler. I have a number of 'go to' recipes for making snacks for the kids' lunchboxes. These recipes are super easy to make and produce a generous amount so they last a few days. Some of my kids' favourites are:

- banana cake

- white chocolate-chip muffins

- Anzac biscuits

- 100s of biscuits.

You can find these on the blog at <www.planningwithkids.com/family-friendly-recipes>.

Keep unbaked biscuit dough in the freezer—works a treat. I often prepare vast amounts at once and freeze the cookie dough in rolls. I can then just get it out, slice it, bake it and we have fresh biscuits.

Marita Beard, mum of two <www.leechbabe.com>

Inspiring lunchbox ideas

With more than 200 school days in a year, it can be easy to run out of ideas for what to put into the kids' lunchboxes. So, as you can see in table 2.5, I created a 'cheat sheet' for two weeks' worth of ideas as a guide for inspiration.

Essential kitchen appliances

There are many small appliances and storage containers you can buy for the kitchen that are supposed to make life easier when it comes to preparing meals. You probably don't need half of them, and it can be difficult to find somewhere to store the bulky appliances. I now have a core that I use regularly and highly recommend to other families:

- *Slow cooker.* I was given one as a wedding present and didn't actually use it for six years. Now I use it almost weekly and love it. It helps you get evening meals ready in the morning with minimal fuss.

Table 2.5: lunchbox inspiration cheat sheet

Item	Monday	Tuesday	Wednesday	Thursday	Friday
Week 1					
Core lunch item	Salad sandwich	Vegemite sandwich	Salad wrap	Ham sandwich	Vegemite sandwich
Whole fruit	Apple	Apple	Apple	Apple	Apple
Veggie sticks	Red capsicum	Cucumber	Red capsicum	Carrot	Celery
Fruit pieces	Watermelon	Grapes	Watermelon	Grapes	Strawberries
Crackers	Water crackers	Rice cakes	Cruskits	Vita-Weats	Rice cakes
Home-baked treat	Banana cake	Banana cake	Banana cake	Chocolate balls	Chocolate balls
Week 2					
Core lunch item	Cold lamb sandwich	Cold lamb sandwich	Vegemite sandwich	Salad sandwich	Salad sandwich
Whole fruit	Pear	Apple	Pear	Apple	Pear
Veggie sticks	Snow peas	Green beans	Snow peas	Green beans	Carrot
Fruit pieces	Mandarin	Orange	Kiwi fruit	Mandarin	Orange
Crackers	Rice cakes	Cruskits	Rice cakes	Cruskits	Water crackers
Home-baked treat	Banana cake	Banana cake	Banana cake	Chocolate cake	Chocolate cake

- *Large double steamer.* This is perfect for cooking large quantities of steamed vegetables and for making vegetable meals for babies when they start solids.

- *Rice cooker.* A rice cooker provides a very quick and easy way to cook large quantities of rice.

- *Large electric frypan.* I choose a non-stick frypan as I find with the heavy usage ours gets, the pan's lifetime is longer. We've found non-stick pans deteriorate quickly (especially if you put them in the dishwasher).

- *Large stockpot.* This is ideal for making large batches of soup or cooking up bulk amounts of pasta.

- *Fridge storage containers.* The secret to keeping fruit and vegetables fresh for the week is not using the crisper sections of the fridge. We keep all fruit and vegetables in specifically designed fridge containers that keep them fresher for much longer periods of time.

- *Pantry storage containers.* These are the most efficient and organised way to store baking goods such as flour, sugar, desiccated coconut and cocoa.

- *Electric mixer.* I'd love a flashy stand mixer, but it's not necessary for the type of cooking I do now. A hand-held electric mixer easily meets my needs.

- *Hand blender.* This is essential for making the kids' favourite soup (pumpkin) and handy for blending food when introducing solids to baby.

Taking action

- Start menu planning.
- Use the monthly menu plan template as a guide for helping build your menu plan.

- Add checklists to your pantry cupboards to keep track of items that need to be replaced.

- Create a shopping routine that allows you to purchase quality produce for the best price.

- Plan and prepare for mealtimes to make them a more enjoyable part of the day.

- Allocate cooking duties to your partner and kids to share the mealtime workload.

- Create a 'family favourites' list of meals that everyone loves as a handy menu-planning reference.

- Create a school lunchbox guide to make the daily task of preparing school lunches easier and more automated.

- Start lunchbox preparation the night before to take the pressure off busy school mornings.

- Allocate a regular time for baking. It makes filling lunchboxes with healthy food so much easier.

- Have the right equipment to make cooking healthy food for your family as easy as possible.

Chapter 3

Family finances

Every parent knows that as your family expands and as children grow, so do the family expenses. There are certain times during the year when I feel we're haemorrhaging cash. The beginning of school terms in particular can be difficult, with payments for after-school activities due, new clothes needed for the change of season and many utility bills also due around this time.

The family budget

Setting up a family budget was the best thing we did to stay on top of our finances. We've been running a family budget since we dropped to one income about eight years ago.

Budgeting is an ongoing activity for us that requires regular review to accommodate expansion and growth. It isn't a task we complete once and forget. As circumstances and requirements alter, the changes in income (hopefully up) and expenses (definitely up) need to be factored in so it truly reflects the household's finances.

Why family budgets work

I'm often asked if building and maintaining a family budget is worth the time it takes. Absolutely, it is! Budgets centralise the information needed to keep the finances under control and they work because they:

- *determine the cash available for spending.* Unless you sit down and calculate total expenses and incoming monies, you really are spending blindly.

- *let you prioritise the family spending.* Rarely are there enough funds for all the purchases you would like to make. Assessing this up front means you can choose what are the most important areas you need to allocate funds to.

- *highlight where your money is being spent.* With cheques, credit cards, cash and regular direct debits, it can be difficult to get a feeling for where all your money is going, unless you track spending.

- *help limit unnecessary expenses.* Budgeting and tracking where you spend your money is like having a second voice: Do I really need this? Is there room in the budget for this?

- *create habits to enable savings.* Once you start budgeting, it quickly becomes evident how even small changes add up over time and can help to build up your savings. I find this really encourages me to keep going and meet a specific goal so we can have that family holiday or buy the new couch.

- *provide an example to the kids of financial responsibility.* Children are heavily influenced by what they see. If all they see is spending, without the backdrop of a budget, they may get a distorted reality of how household finances work.

Our biggest [rule] when it comes to spending is if we NEED it we get it, if we WANT it we don't (it goes on a wish list).

Brooke, mum of one

How to set a family budget

The easiest way to set a family budget is to break it down into a series of concrete steps (see figure 3.1).

1   Record all sources of income and expenses (fixed and variable) on the basis of frequency and amount.

2   Determine an annual savings goal (revisit step 1 if necessary).

3   Track daily spending.

4   Review progress of performance (revisit step 1 if necessary).

Figure 3.1: family budget flow chart

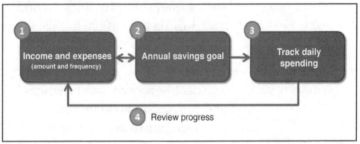

It helps to work on these steps one at a time so you don't feel overwhelmed by all the information to be collected. A simple spreadsheet is an effective tool for organising this information. Microsoft's Excel package is the most well known brand of spreadsheet, but if you don't have access to it there's a range of free online versions available on the internet, such as Google Docs. Google Docs is a really effective tool for tracking spending across multiple locations (work and home) and across multiple people (both parents).

What helps us a lot is [that] my partner has another spreadsheet as well as the family budget. It tracks the progress on our mortgage (payments made, interest charged, and how far ahead we are of the bank's 'scheduled' total). The second motivates a keen adherence to the first, because money we preserve by keeping to our budget goes straight off the mortgage in almost all cases and we can SEE the benefit of that very clearly.

Kathryn Sinclair, mum of three
<www.playeatlearnlive.blogspot.com>

The basis of this approach to budgeting is to review the whole year, then break down the regular components on the basis of amount and frequency. This ensures you have enough cash to:

* enjoy the lifestyle you want and can afford

* put some away for a rainy day (for example, if the fridge has a heart attack or for an annual holiday) and to cover the 'lumpy' periods in the year.

You can find a template for a family budget spreadsheet at <www.planningwithkids.com/resources>. The template allows you to enter and record your income and expenses (step 1), target an annual savings goal (step 2) and track daily spending (step 3).

Step 1: estimate your income and expenses

Income: You need to estimate the total income for the year. This figure needs to include all sources of income, such as paid employment, government benefits, and returns on any investments the family receives and their frequency, as shown in table 3.1.

Table 3.1: income (example figures)

	INPUT amount	INPUT frequency	Yearly total
Salary (or wage)	$2 500	26	$65 000
Family benefits (social security)	$100	12	$1 200

If you have a regular salaried income, the process for entering the regular after-tax income multiplied by the period is very simple ($500 × 52 weeks, or $1000 × 26 weeks, or $2167 × 12 months). If your salary varies a lot from week to week, consider an average amount you believe to be realistic, or a minimum amount (if you want to be ultra conservative). If your income is seasonal, include the number of weeks you work multiplied by the amount ($700 × 12 weeks, for example).

Expenses (fixed): Recording your expenses takes more time than recording your income because we all have many expense transactions over the course of a week, month or year. While some expenses are fixed and some are variable, it will probably surprise you to see how many fit into the former category, and how large they are as well.

The first step is to detail all the fixed payments you have throughout the year. These costs define your financial life. If you purchase a $10 bunch of roses every week, this should be included in your budget. If purchasing a coffee every morning is a mandatory, not-negotiable, must-have event in your day, then include $3.50 every day for 365 days a year. (However, if you *occasionally* purchase a second coffee, this will need to be recorded as variable spending.)

With utility spending (such as gas, electricity and phone), many providers have offers for 'smoothing' seasonal bills. This makes the budgeting process and cash flow easier. However, if these bills can't be smoothed, have a look at your bills for the past 12 months. For example, if you spent $300 on gas bills last winter, then it's highly likely you'll spend a similar amount this winter. If the actual figure is 10 per cent more, that's when step 2 (determining an annual savings goal) is used to accommodate the uncertainties. If you don't have last year's records and you want to complete your budget now, you can either call your provider for this information or make an estimate and then update your budget as you receive the bills. Understanding the large items is important so you can manage the smaller, variable expenses with confidence.

Table 3.2 (overleaf) shows how your fixed expenses might look. Once you've calculated your yearly fixed expenses, you have a figure that will help determine what your maximum variable (discretionary) spending can be. The figure highlighted in bold in table 3.2 is then included in your net yearly savings calculations (see table 3.3 on p. 65) to determine what your maximum weekly variable spending amount must be if you want to achieve your yearly savings goal. If this figure is positive, hooray for you! If you stick to your budget you'll save money in that year. If it's negative and your expenses are higher than your income for the year, there are three options available to you:

- Dip into your savings.
- Pull back on some of your fixed or variable spending.
- Find some way of increasing your income.

Table 3.2: fixed expenses (example figures)

	Total	Jul.	Aug.	Sep.	Oct.	Nov.	Dec.	Jan.	Feb.	Mar.	Apr.	May	Jun.
Utilities													
Water	$400			$100			$100			$100		$100	
Telephone	$1 000			$250			$250			$250			$250
Gas and electricity	$1 080	$90	$90	$90	$90	$90	$90	$90	$90	$90	$90	$90	$90
Internet	$420	$35	$35	$35	$35	$35	$35	$35	$35	$35	$35	$35	$35
Financial													
Mortgage (or rent)	$12 000	$1 000	$1 000	$1 000	$1 000	$1 000	$1 000	$1 000	$1 000	$1 000	$1 000	$1 000	$1 000
Accountant fees	$250								$250				
Bank fees	$300						$300						
Pocket money	$480	$40	$40	$40	$40	$40	$40	$40	$40	$40	$40	$40	$40
Education													
School fees	$800	$200			$200				$200			$200	
Kinder fees	$1 440		$360			$360			$360			$360	
Insurance													
Car	$600							$600					
House	$300		$300										

Family finances

	Total	Jul.	Aug.	Sep.	Oct.	Nov.	Dec.	Jan.	Feb.	Mar.	Apr.	May	Jun.
Contents	$550		$550										
Health	$2 400	$200	$200	$200	$200	$200	$200	$200	$200	$200	$200	$200	$200
Travel													
Car registration	$500							$500					
Car maintenance	$400			$400									
Auto club	$75	$75											
Public transport	$1 200	$100	$100	$100	$100	$100	$100	$100	$100	$100	$100	$100	$100
Miscellaneous													
Newspaper	$240	$20	$20	$20	$20	$20	$20	$20	$20	$20	$20	$20	$20
Milk delivery	$480	$40	$40	$40	$40	$40	$40	$40	$40	$40	$40	$40	$40
Dog fees	$40									$40			
Rates	$800		$200			$200			$200			$200	
Gym membership	$720	$60	$60	$60	$60	$60	$60	$60	$60	$60	$60	$60	$60
Presents—general	$636	$53	$53	$53	$53	$53	$53	$53	$53	$53	$53	$53	$53
Presents—Christmas	$1 000						$1 000						
$28 105 ← This figure links into the 'Net yearly savings' worksheet (table 3.3).													

If I had my time over I would not worry so much about buying everything new for my first baby. It was a huge expense at a time when the bills were just about to escalate. eBay is such an amazing way to source everything needed to set up your home—and you can always find things that are still in excellent condition for a fraction of the new price.

Catherine Sangster, mum of three
<www.keepcatebusy.blogspot.com>

Expenses (variable): Your variable expenses are all of the other things (apart from your fixed, regular expenses) you spend your money on. They include groceries, clothes, petrol, entertainment, children's activities, that second takeaway coffee and much more. It's difficult to categorise each of these expenses individually, so to keep it simple we use three core discretionary expenditure categories. It's important to keep this simple so that completing the third budgeting step—tracking daily spending—is a quick and easy task. We use these categories:

- *Groceries.* As well as food, this also includes nappies, toiletries and any additional items bought from the supermarket.

- *Miscellaneous expenses.* This is the catch-all category for those expenses that don't fit into the groceries or clothes categories. It includes things such as out-of-pocket medical expenses, babysitting, petrol, takeaway coffees, takeaway dinners and swimming lessons.

- *Clothes.* This is the category where you'll see the most variation because it's not a regular weekly expenditure. In our family we tend to buy clothes at the change of seasons and in bulk, so we may go for weeks without spending on clothes, but when we do, we spend $300 on winter jackets for all five kids—or much more if my husband buys a new suit for work.

It can appear incorrect to define groceries as a variable expense because we all have to eat. When shopping for groceries, however, there is considerable choice as to what we buy, how much we buy and where we buy from. Therefore, we use our discretion to make the purchases that are right for our family. For example, the chocolates that make their way regularly onto my shopping list are completely discretionary. I could definitely live without them! I don't want to though, so I buy them and they form part of my grocery spending.

The most effective way to determine the budget for variable expenses is to note all your discretionary expenditure over a few weeks. Write down everything, come up with a 'best guess' of what you will spend, and then multiply this by a frequency of 52 weeks for the year.

Table 3.3: net yearly savings (example figures)

	INPUT amount	INPUT frequency	Yearly total
Income			
Salary (or wage)	$2500	26	$65000
Family benefits (social security)	$100	12	$1200
Investments	$500	12	$6000
			$72200
Expenses			
Regular payments (i.e. bills, train fares, insurances)	$28105	1	$28105
Groceries	$275	52	$14300
Miscellaneous expenses	$275	52	$14300
Clothes	$100	52	$5200
			$61905
Net yearly savings (or deficit)			**$10295**

Step 2: determine your yearly savings goal

In the first step we determined our income and our fixed and variable expenses. The next step is to plan for future expenditure. Once all of these items have been entered, the spreadsheet calculates the net yearly savings (or deficit). In table 3.3, the result is $10 295 in savings. This is generally not the case the first time you put together a budget.

When we did our first budget, we estimated a significant deficit. This really scared me. It became very clear I was on a spending path that was going to get us into financial trouble. It was the small things that added up: morning tea with friends, magazines, buying 'on-sale' clothing. Setting a budget didn't mean I couldn't spend money on these things, but it did teach me that I needed to make more considered decisions.

To reduce the estimated deficit, we looked at all of our expenses and worked out where we could make cuts. We had to make changes to our lifestyle to do this. For the first couple of years our goal was simply to break even.

Knowing your forecast financial situation is incredibly useful. If you wanted to save for a home deposit or a new car, you may need a $10 000 surplus to achieve your goal. Through the budget-setting process you can determine the areas of spending you need to reduce or eliminate. You're then aware of any lifestyle changes you need to make, which ultimately makes achieving your financial goals much more likely. The hardest part of the budget process is setting it up the first time. Adjusting the budget for the changes in your life is much simpler from then on.

Step 3: track your daily spending

For budgeting to be effective, you need to now match your well-researched and considered set of numbers with the discipline to track your spending and review your performance. Without this, a budget is just a meaningless set of numbers on a page.

My husband and I both access a computer most days so entering every transaction into the tracking worksheet is convenient for us. This is where Google Docs is incredibly flexible. We uploaded our spreadsheet to Google Docs and we can access it on any computer with internet access. However, you don't have to use a computer to track expenditure. For the first year or two of tracking our expenses, we handwrote all expenses on a printed pro-forma spreadsheet and then added up the totals weekly.

A template for tracking daily expenditure is shown in table 3.4 (overleaf) and in the family budget spreadsheet found at <www.planningwithkids.com/resources>. There you'll also find a link to a Google Docs spreadsheet template.

In table 3.4 you can see just how quick and easy it is to start running a deficit. This is especially the case when you first begin the tracking process. We do our grocery shopping monthly, but the budget is based on weekly expenditure. This means our weekly spending varies quite significantly on paper for expenses such as groceries and clothes. It's much better to look at the overall trend of the budget. If we're simply adding to the deficit every week, then something is wrong and needs to be addressed.

Personally, the greatest benefit of regularly tracking our expenses is that it makes me think twice about spending our money. For example, the first week in table 3.4 (overleaf) shows a deficit of $425. This information allows me to make a considered decision. I wouldn't choose that weekend to take the kids to the movies. Instead, we might have a movie night at home: watch a DVD with popcorn and rearrange the lounge room to make it more special.

Table 3.4: tracking daily spending (example figures)

| 2011 | Input daily spend here ($) | | | Variance to budget ($) | | | | |
	Misc.	Groceries	Clothes	275 Misc.	275 Groceries	100 Clothes	Total	
Mon, 2 May	10	400						
Tue, 3 May	107	6	50					
Wed, 4 May		12						
Thu, 5 May	10							
Fri, 6 May	300			527	498	50	1075	Week total
Sat, 7 May	80	60		−252	−223	50	−425	Variance to budget
Sun, 8 May	20	20		−252	−223	50	−425	Total position (…this is the most important number)
Mon, 9 May	13							
Tue, 10 May	80	22						
Wed, 11 May	12							
Thu, 12 May		6						
Fri, 13 May	40			145	88	0	233	Week total
Sat, 14 May		60		130	187	100	417	Variance to budget
Sun, 15 May				−122	−36	150	−8	Total position (…this is the most important number)

| 2011 | Input daily spend here ($) | | | Variance to budget ($) | | | | |
	Misc.	Groceries	Clothes	275 Misc.	275 Groceries	100 Clothes	Total	
Mon, 16 May		430						
Tue, 17 May	22							
Wed, 18 May		15						
Thu, 19 May	50	7						
Fri, 20 May				72	512	200	784	Week total
Sat, 21 May		60	200	203	−237	−100	−134	Variance to budget
Sun, 22 May				81	−273	50	−142	Total position (…this is the most important number)
Mon, 23 May		32						
Tue, 24 May	90							
Wed, 25 May	80	6						
Thu, 26 May	30							
Fri, 27 May		6		225	104	0	329	Week total
Sat, 28 May	25	60		50	171	100	321	Variance to budget
Sun, 29 May				131	−102	150	179	Total position (…this is the most important number)

It's also important not to run a zero balance each week. For example, the allocation for clothing in the table is $100 a week, but, in reality, this is not how expenditure on clothes works. A new suit for my husband or replenishing the school uniforms at the start of the year costs significantly more than the weekly allocation. In the weeks leading up to purchasing these items, we need to start building a surplus to keep the budget on track.

Step 4: review your progress

By entering your daily spending, you can instantly view the health of your budget. In addition, it's important to review your overall budget regularly to make sure it remains relevant and realistic, and that it addresses any areas of overspending. When we first started budgeting, we would review our budget each quarter. Some of our initial estimates on spending in areas such as groceries weren't reflecting reality. We were spending at least $50 a week more than we thought we had been. We allocated more money to the budget for groceries, but as the budget was only just balanced, we had to find somewhere to take the money from. It came from miscellaneous expenditure. This then meant a further tightening up on things such as those extra coffees here and there, beginning to handmake gifts for people, and changing our newspaper delivery to weekends only.

Now we review the budget during the year on an as-needs basis. Over the years we've been able to accurately estimate our spending on groceries and clothes. The 'miscellaneous' category continues to be the trickiest one to balance as it covers expenditure on unpredictable costs. By having a budget, and tracking and reviewing our progress, it's been possible for us to reduce our debt to only having a mortgage while still buying the essential, additional big items (such as a fridge) when we need them and taking the occasional family holiday!

Managing pocket money

You might have noticed in table 3.2 that one of the fixed expenses we budget for is pocket money for the kids. This is not a necessity, but we made a decision that we would give pocket money to our kids to teach them practical finance lessons such as:

- *the value of money:* for example, understanding the cost of items and toys

- *decision making:* how best to use their limited funds

- *saving:* setting themselves goals — both short- and long-term — for how they'll spend their money

- *not being influenced by advertising:* when they see something in a catalogue or on TV and they say they want to spend their pocket money on it, this is the perfect opportunity to explain the purpose of advertising, and how to question what they're hearing and reading

- *social etiquette:* learning to be discreet about their earnings and being grateful for what they receive.

Pocket-money guidelines

When we decided we'd give our children pocket money, I did quite a bit of research. I wanted to understand the different models used and to find one that would fit in with our parenting style.

As with most parenting information, I found many pocket-money models, so our model is a hybrid of what I liked best about the various models I read about. In short, this is what my husband and I came up with.

- We would hand out pocket money fortnightly.

- It would be given out at the end of family meetings. If we missed a family meeting for some reason, the kids would receive the owed money at the next meeting.

- The amount would differ according to the children's ages.

- Once they reached school age, each child would get an increase. The additional amount was to be deposited into their school bank account.

- The children may not spend their money until they've saved $20.

- The children may choose how to spend their money.

- Pocket money is not related to their allocated jobs around the house.

We don't attach pocket money to chores, but they have money they can 'earn' by doing extra. It is their share of the household income just as housework is their share of the household care. Privileges are withdrawn for lack of household help though. Things like TV/PC/game [console] time. We use a timer too, and if the job is taking longer than expected we time in a break or two.

Bettina Purdie, mum of three <www.robecriluto.com>

When to start giving pocket money

We chose to start giving our eldest son pocket money when he started school at age five. Before that we didn't feel he needed his own supply of cash! However, we started giving our second son a very small amount of pocket money after he turned three so he wouldn't feel left out. This decision made shopping trips designed for spending pocket money much easier!

How much pocket money?

I don't think there is any 'right' amount to give kids in terms of pocket money. It's a relative issue determined by your family's income. I understand that for some families giving pocket money isn't even an option as there's simply no room for it in the budget. My biggest tip for handing out pocket money is to start small and make sure your family budget can cope with this regular payment.

I have a seven, nine and 11 year old. They [each] get $1 a week. Kids today get way too much—they buy, buy, buy. It's important for children to learn to save and consider their purchases, just like we have to.

Georgina Rechner, mum of three

It's also important to be clear on what we, as parents, don't expect the kids to have to spend their pocket money on. We give only a small amount of pocket money, but we pay for things such as the kids' trips out with friends and the occasional treat from the school canteen. Other families choose to give a much larger amount, but expect their kids to manage their money and pay for extra items as well.

Our eldest son started secondary school recently, and he takes public transport to school. We're going to trial the second method mentioned above as we think it's more appropriate for his circumstances and age. Parenting kids is a dynamic task requiring constant adaptation, modification and reality checks!

Spending pocket money

We'd agreed that the kids needed to save at least $20 before they could spend any money to ensure they didn't get caught up in constant consumerism and instant gratification. It also meant they could buy one bigger item as opposed to a few smaller items. Stuff already accumulates so quickly in our house that we didn't want to exacerbate this even further.

We'd also agreed that the kids could choose what they spent their money on, but I have to admit to initially trying to influence their purchases. If they were looking at a commercialised toy that made noises and needed batteries, I would — not so innocently — try to distract their attention to an educational game! I didn't get away with this for very long as my eldest son, who was seven at the time, soon worked out what I was doing. He made it clear that it was 'my money and I get to decide'. He was right: if I was going to encourage responsible spending, I had to allow them to make their own choices.

The first year our kids were given pocket money, they bought a lot of plastic, junky toys. This was most likely a direct result of my not having ever bought these types of toys for them, and for a while it seemed it was all they were interested in.

However, I only had to put up with these toys for a relatively short time because allowing the kids to buy them actually resulted in a positive longer term outcome. As the kids grew older and become more experienced at spending their money, they worked out for themselves that these cheap, plastic toys weren't that great after all: they broke easily and many small parts were difficult to keep track of.

Once they learned this, the older kids started putting more thought into their purchases. They started setting savings goals of more than $20 because they had particular items in mind. The items they spend their pocket money on now are rarely toys. Books, cricket gear, a hammock and an umbrella are among the purchases they have planned and made.

Taking action

- Create a family budget.

- Use the budget template to help you determine your expenses and the level of savings you want to aim for.

- Begin tracking your daily expenditure, using either the template spreadsheet or a notebook.

- If you already have a budget in place, take the time to regularly review and modify it so it can help you meet your family's financial goals.

- Decide whether to give your kids pocket money.

- If you're going to give pocket money, spend time defining why you want to and create a process for doing so.

Part II
Ages and stages

Chapter 4

Navigating with a new baby

When you're having your first baby, there's time to prepare and plan for the new arrival. (Thankfully, babies give you a bit of notice that they're on their way!) As you have more children, daily life can often already be busy, leaving little time to prepare for a new baby. However, I've found taking even a small amount of time to prepare yourself and your family pays great dividends in the long run.

As I worked four days a week until a month before the birth of my second child, I didn't spend much time at all on getting organised. I didn't have a freezer stocked with meals, or menu plans prepared to get me through the blur that is the initial few weeks with an infant. We coped—we muddled through—but I began to see ways I could have better prepared our home for his arrival. And with each beautiful baby, I implemented ways to better prepare the whole family for our newest addition. My greatest success came from building some of the preparation into my everyday routines so that it didn't actually seem like so much extra work.

Getting organised for the birth

There are hundreds of books that will tell you all the things you need to buy for you and your newborn baby, but I haven't found many of these necessary at all. My advice to new mums is to not feel you have to have everything. Babies need very little bought 'stuff'. But don't think that I wasn't captivated by the baby books and didn't head out and spend a mini fortune on things that I eventually didn't use, because I did. With each baby I've used less stuff. I've gradually worked out what makes life easier for me, bubs and the rest of the family. The items I consider essential for newborns are:

- nappies and wipes
- nappy-rash cream
- cloth nappies or clean-up cloths
- bath oil or wash
- sorbolene
- clothes
- a bassinet
- a cot
- a baby capsule
- a baby carrier
- muslin wraps.

These are the items I consider essential for mums during the late stages of pregnancy and the first few weeks post-birth:

- a hot/cold pack

- maternity pads

- nursing pads

- comfy clothes

- bike shorts

- a baby bag

- an express pump for breastfeeding

- a reusable water bottle.

Preparing the kids for a new baby

Kids cope best when they know what to expect, so it's worth spending time preparing children for the arrival of their future sibling. This doesn't need to be a serious event. Involving your kids in planning for the baby's arrival can include activities such as:

- *setting up the baby's bassinet.* Allow your toddler or preschooler to help you. Talk about how much babies sleep during the day and how they wake up overnight. Let them know that Mum will need to wake up overnight too and may be tired for a little while after the baby is born.

- *making meals in advance.* Allow your older kids to help you cook. Talk about how the new baby may be unsettled in the early evenings and how having meals in the freezer to go will help make life easier on days when the baby doesn't sleep so well. Explain how they will need to use their time wisely when the baby is sleeping to do reading and homework activities.

- *washing baby clothes.* Have your younger children help you hang out and fold up the baby clothes. Talk about the size of the clothes and how babies are very little when they're born. Discuss how babies need lots of attention from Mum and Dad for feeding, changing, settling and bathing and how there will be lots of ways they can help Mum and Dad look after the baby.

- *looking at baby photos.* Spend some time with your children looking through their baby photos. As you look through the photos, tell them their birth stories and the lovely memories you have of them as infants. Talk about how they liked to be soothed when they were upset and the special things you did with them.

Roleplay and books

In addition to using real-life experiences to prepare your kids for a new baby, you can also use roleplay and books. Roleplay can be a fun way to give younger children an idea of what it will be like to have a new baby in the house. Set up a play area with a doll, a doll's bed and other accessories. If you have only one child, ask the child to take on a role. They could be the mum, the dad or themselves. Play out common situations that will happen when baby arrives, such as a preschooler wanting to play a game and the baby needing settling.

Books can provide another avenue for getting kids thinking about what it will be like with a new baby in the house. Some fabulous books for toddlers and preschoolers are:

- *Hey Hippopotamus, Do Babies Eat Cake Too?* by Hazel Edwards
- *Brand New Baby* by Bob Graham
- *Za-Za's Baby Brother* by Lucy Cousins
- *I Want a Sister* by Tony Ross
- *There's a House Inside My Mummy* by Giles Andreae
- *It's Quacking Time!* by Martin Waddell.

Increasing kids' independence

I've always tried to use the time before the birth of a new baby to work on age-appropriate independence skills with my kids. It can be easy to do things for younger kids that they're actually capable of doing themselves because it's quicker and easier to do it for them at the time. However, with the feeding and time demands of a new little one, it's incredibly helpful if the kids can do more for themselves.

Teaching kids age-appropriate independence skills before the baby is born means they won't connect this directly to the arrival of their new sibling. It also means that you won't have to try teaching the kids these skills while carrying a baby around and suffering from sleep deprivation.

Changing routines

When bringing a new baby into the house, the family dynamics always receive a bit of a shake-up, regardless of how well you've prepared. So this is not the ideal time to try to change the kids' routines. I found making adjustments to their daily routines a month or two before the baby arrives more successful. Here are a couple of changes you might like to consider:

- *From cot to bed.* Changing a toddler's sleeping place is exciting for them. My kids took a week or so to adapt to sleeping in a bed that they could get out of whenever they felt like it. Making the change before the birth of the baby meant I had time to work with my toddlers on staying in bed once we had turned out the lights. This also helps prevent any displacement children may feel if they're concerned about the baby taking their place.

- *Toilet training.* This requires much time and patience, and can result in a lot of extra washing. If toddlers are ready to be toilet trained before baby is born, then seize the opportunity. I don't, however, recommend forcing the issue if the toddler isn't ready. Our first son showed signs that he was ready for toilet training so we decided to try it a couple of months before our second child was due. After a week of no nappies and continual accidents, we decided that he wasn't ready. The nappies went back on and we waited until a few months after the baby was born before trying again, so I could give the process enough attention and the toddler enough support. He was almost three by the time he was toilet trained: not only was he ready, but so was I, and within a week he was successfully toilet trained.

Preparing friends and family

I've been lucky to have a supportive family and wonderful friends who offered to help when our babies were born. I'm not always good at accepting help: sometimes I like to think I can do it all myself. This thought process is wrong on two basic levels:

- I possibly could do it all myself, but I'd be doing so at a cost—I'd be sacrificing sleep and time bonding with my new baby.

- It doesn't recognise the feelings of others who genuinely want to be part of this time in our life.

Building up credits

With each child, I've accepted more help from family and friends. However, I don't like this to be a one-way street.

In the lead-up to the birth of the baby I'll make sure I'm actively helping others whenever I can. It doesn't mean I exhaust myself doing work for others, but it means I look for opportunities in my daily life where I can help—for example:

- dropping a friend's children home from school

- having toddlers or preschoolers over to play for a few hours in the morning so Mum has time to run errands or attend appointments

- having family over for dinner on the weekend when my husband is home

- cooking a double batch of a basic meal such as spaghetti bolognaise, and giving one portion to a friend who has a new baby herself.

I see this as building up credits. I know my friends and family don't expect this of me, but it's something I like to do. For someone like me who finds it difficult to ask for help, it makes me feel a little more comfortable.

My pregnancies have all been trouble-free, and I've maintained excellent health throughout each of them. This isn't the case for all mums-to-be, so you may not be in a position to take on these kinds of activities when you're pregnant, and you actually may need more help during this time. It may be that you feel you need assistance from family and friends during your pregnancy, and they're sure to understand and be willing to help, so don't be afraid to ask for assistance if you need it.

Practical baby gifts

Family and friends are always generous when it comes to gift giving for a new baby. I'm continually surprised at how much we receive. When we had our first child, our family and friends would frequently ask whether there was anything we 'needed' that they could buy us as a gift. Just as I did with asking for help, I also struggled a little with suggesting gift ideas. I felt it sounded a bit rude and demanding. On the flip side, though, I love it when I ask people the same question and they run off a couple of things they'd like.

The birth of a baby is the perfect time for practical gifts. Many families—including ours—are affected by the adjustment to one income and ever-increasing expenses. While beautiful and expensive clothes for baby are lovely, they only last a short time. It wasn't until we had babies four and five that I actually started giving my family ideas for practical gifts, when they asked, such as a new hand mixer (for pureeing food, as our old one had broken) and a new baby bag (as the old one was worn out).

There are many practical items that family and close friends can purchase for you when you have a new baby. Here are some ideas to get you thinking:

- cloth nappies, not only for baby's bottom, but perfect for cleaning up baby's mess

- a toddler seat or buggy board attachment for your pram

- a large double steamer for cooking up baby's veggies

- a rice cooker: this makes cooking rice and making risottos so easy, with less mess

- a big clothes horse (in winter it can be impossible to dry anything outside in Melbourne!)

- a microwave steriliser for sterilising baby's bottles quickly and easily.

Preparing food

Serving up a nutritious family meal on time can be difficult when you have a newborn. Including meal preparation as part of my routine in the lead-up to the birth of each baby made this task easier.

Cooking in bulk

Most pregnancy books tell you to cook some meals in advance and have them in the freezer for when baby is born. It sounds easy, but in reality, towards the end of a pregnancy tiredness can hit, and even serving up an evening meal for the family can be a challenge in itself. Preparing a simple, bulk-cooking schedule can really help make this task doable. It makes it part of your daily routine rather than a separate task that has to be added to the 'to do' list.

For some meals—such as lasagne—you'll have leftovers even when you cook the standard quantity. Instead of eating the leftovers for lunch or another meal, begin freezing these portions over a couple of months and you'll soon have enough in the freezer for extra meals. Other meals—such as pumpkin soup and spaghetti bolognaise—are easy to cook in double quantities so you can freeze one full serve. Try following these steps to help get you started on building your freezer supplies.

- Find out which meals your family likes that freeze well.

- Work out the freezer life of these meals (for example, beef stroganoff will last for about three months and lasagne about two months).

- Schedule preparing and freezing these meals into your menu plans in the months leading up to the birth of your baby.

- Either freeze them as a family-sized meal or in individual adult or child portions.

The pre-baby, bulk-cooking plan shown in table 4.1 is an example of a cooking schedule that would provide you with a combination of full-sized family meals and leftover portions in your freezer. Each of these meals can be added to the weekly menu plan for that week so that the extra cooking fits easily into that part of your day. A template for this checklist can be found at <www.planningwithkids.com/resources>.

Table 4.1: pre-baby bulk-cooking plan

Date	Meal	Freezer life
8 weeks to go	Beef curry—double recipe	Approx. 4 months
7 weeks to go	Pumpkin soup—double recipe	Approx. 4 months
6 weeks to go	Tomato soup—double recipe	Approx. 4 months
5 weeks to go	Beef stroganoff—double recipe	Approx. 3 months
4 weeks to go	Chicken lasagne—individual portions from leftovers	Approx. 3 months
3 weeks to go	Bolognaise sauce—double recipe	Approx. 3 months
2 weeks to go	Lasagne—individual portions from leftovers	Approx. 2 months
1 week to go	Chicken lasagne—individual portions from leftovers	Approx. 3 months

Menu planning in advance

Unless you have an amazingly large freezer that you can stockpile with tons of prepared meals, the reality is that you'll still have to cook meals most days of the week when you have a newborn. In chapter 2, I shared a monthly menu-planning template. If you're not into regular menu planning yet, a couple of weeks before your due date take the time to prepare a month of menu plans. The meals don't have to be assigned to any permanent dates, but you can plan them for a four-week period so that you'll have a weekly menu plan for you and others to follow and a grocery shopping list for each week that anyone can shop from. This will help you through the mealtime workload, whenever your beautiful baby decides to arrive.

Menu plans can really help with sharing the workload when baby needs your attention the most. My husband is a pretty good shopper if he has a list. When our last baby was born, we had six weeks of menu plans and associated shopping lists hanging on a clip on the fridge. He went to the market each weekend to buy the fresh fruit and vegetables using these lists and made a trip to the supermarket once a fortnight. It was fabulous not to have to think about the planning and shopping for meals for a few weeks knowing that we had everything we needed.

Stocking up on essentials

When you have more than one child, it's hard to have a set routine for a new baby. They're frequently lugged in and out of the car during the run-around that takes place due to their siblings' requirements. Prior to my due date for the last two babies I stocked up on necessary items for the house that I knew would eventually be used or consumed. This helped cut out trips to the shops with a newborn, meaning baby's routine was less interrupted and I wasn't so busy. I had a checklist that ensured the following household areas were well stocked:

- pantry
- fridge

- freezer
- medicine cabinet
- toiletries
- kids' socks
- cleaning products
- laundry products.

Preparing for celebrations

Two of our babies were born close to Christmas. I made sure I had all the Christmas shopping done a couple of weeks before my due date. I'm not a fan of shopping in crowds anytime, especially not when I have a newborn baby. I take a similar approach with birthday presents: I write up a list of upcoming birthdays for the three months following baby's arrival and determine the presents I need to buy. I then purchase them (and the cards) so they're ready in time for each birthday.

Investigate delivery services; shopping with a newborn can be hard work. There are many companies that offer free delivery of basics such as nappies, fruit and veggies, meat, milk and bread. Most of the big supermarkets have online shopping too, which allows you to have everything delivered.

Lou Woods, mum of four

Preparing baby's clothes

I boxed up baby clothes as each baby outgrew theirs: a boys' box, a girls' box and a 'neutral' box. We chose not to find out the sex of our babies, which meant organising baby clothes required a bit of preparation. Before each baby was born I would wash all the baby clothes, placing the neutral clothes in baby's drawers (and some in the hospital bag). Then we'd wait to see what other clothes we'd need.

Preparing the hospital bag

With each pregnancy I've streamlined the task of packing my hospital bag. For the last two pregnancies I created a list of items I'd need to pack into my hospital bag at the last minute. There were a number of things I wanted to pack that I was still using regularly and needed to have available. To make sure they weren't forgotten in the last-minute packing, I found it helpful to have a descriptive list of these items so they could be packed easily once labour started. While I managed my labour, my husband was able to go around ticking off the items on the list while putting them in my hospital bag.

My checklist for our fifth baby is shown in table 4.2 (overleaf). A template for this checklist can be found at <www. planningwithkids.com/resources>.

Small gifts for the kids

We have a tradition that the second time the kids come to visit their new sibling in hospital we give them a small gift on behalf of the new baby. We leave it until the second visit as we want the first one to be solely about introducing them to the special addition to the family.

When the baby is born, it's an exciting time for a family. There are many presents and much attention for the new baby. The small gift is a way of diffusing some of the envy that may result when the other children, mainly the toddler or preschooler, see this. We've always chosen gifts that can entertain the kids while they visit the baby and me in hospital — for example, a book, a story CD, playing cards or an activity or puzzle book.

Table 4.2: hospital bag packing checklist

Item	Location
iPod and iPod dock (check that the cords are there as well)	Your iPod and eldest son's dock (in his room)
Aromatherapy oil burner and essential oils	Kitchen bench
Thongs	Back door shoe shelf
Lemonade	Fridge
Hairdryer	My bathroom cupboard
Bras—two bone and one black	My second drawer
Brown dress	Ironing basket or my wardrobe
Black and grey leggings	My third drawer
Pink water bottle	Kitchen bench

When baby comes home

We're considerably blessed to have five healthy and beautiful children. I've learned an enormous amount with each child and gained more confidence in myself as a mother along the way. Some of the things I know now I wish I'd known when I had my first and second babies. Each baby has their own personality and I found there's always a period of adjustment for the whole family, but particularly for Mum. It can take some time to get back into the swing of things and work out new ways of managing family life with a larger brood. Preparing for this and discussing it with the kids before the baby comes along can help set up the right expectations of what life will be like with a newborn.

However, even when I'm prepared I find I still need specific strategies during this wonderful but exhausting time.

Tip

Coping with a new baby

Enjoying baby

'Coping with a new baby' can sound like babies are only hard work, but this is definitely not the case. They're hard work, but work that reaps amazing results. I've learned babies are small for such a short time that I need to make sure I enjoy that time. This wasn't always easy, and I've had to remind myself that the house would eventually become tidy, the baby would eventually sleep and eventually I wouldn't constantly be in a sleep-deprived fog. The baby, however, would grow up quickly, and that precious time can't be made up.

Trusting your instincts

It's important to trust your knowledge and be confident that you know your baby. I'd try what I thought might work for my baby, and used only the strategies I was comfortable with.

Filtering advice from others

Everybody has advice for new parents. I've always listened to the advice of other parents as they could have useful insights for me. I did, however, filter advice that didn't fit our parenting style. Naturally, we didn't have a parenting style when we started out, but if I tried something and it didn't feel right or made me anxious or worried, I wouldn't keep doing it. It's important to feel comfortable and confident about how you parent your baby.

What sleeping problem?

Someone once gave me this piece of advice on babies and sleeping: 'It's only a sleeping problem if you're unhappy with the sleeping situation'.

When you're deprived of sleep, it's very easy to become slightly obsessed about how much your baby is sleeping (I can speak

Coping with a new baby (*cont'd*)

from personal experience). Lots of people have views on where baby should sleep, how long baby should sleep and when baby should start sleeping through the night. In reality, I don't believe there's any one 'right' way to approach baby's sleep pattern. Don't worry what other people think: if you're happy with how you and baby are sleeping, don't feel pressured to change.

Communicating with your partner

Don't assume your partner knows what you're feeling or what your day was like. Don't keep your feelings to yourself. I've found if I did, the result was a rather big eruption of feelings because there are too many to hold in!

Preparing in advance

Doing things in advance when I had the time meant if everything started to fall apart later in the day, I wouldn't feel so stressed. Cooking the evening meal in the morning is a great example. Late afternoon and early evening can be a challenging time with a new baby, so if you don't have to worry about cooking, you can spend more time tending to baby's needs.

Taking nana naps

I love an afternoon nap. Lying down for an afternoon nap when my baby and toddler were having their afternoon sleeps was critical for keeping my sanity. It meant that by the time the rush hit at 5 pm I wasn't completely exhausted and I had more patience for the kids.

Readjusting your standards

Depending on how much your baby sleeps and how you've recovered from the birth, you may need to adjust your standards on things such as ironing, cleaning and fancy meals. I would stick to a 'keep it simple' approach for the first few months, including easy meals that the kids love (even if that meant having spaghetti bolognaise once a week).

Getting out of the house

Exercise and fresh air are great for you and the baby. I found going for a walk each day did wonders for my mood. As it can be quite isolating being home with a baby, having a playgroup or a regular social outlet with adult stimulation through the week can be a refreshing change too.

Acknowledging your work

When you have a newborn, it's important to acknowledge all the things you've managed to achieve every day. It can be easy to focus on what didn't get done (like the pile of washing to be folded or the floors that need a mop). If I managed to get the children to school on time, cooked an evening meal and played with the baby and preschooler, it was a great day. Life with a new baby is a time when just completing the essential tasks is a great achievement.

Entertaining the toddler while breastfeeding

The age gap between each of our children and the next one is roughly the same (about two and a half years). This has meant we've always had a newborn and a toddler at the one time. In the early weeks, when the newborn is breastfeeding frequently, I've found it helpful to be prepared in terms of entertainment for the toddler. While you're sitting and feeding the baby the house can be a potential danger zone if a toddler is unoccupied for too long.

I had a special box for my toddler when the baby was born. It only came out when I fed the baby, and went back in the cupboard after feeding finished. I rotated small toys and art activities—bouncy ball, write-and-wipe boards, stickers, puzzles and so on.

Karen Comer, mum of three
<www.earthlyjoyride.blogspot.com>

I found a few low-key ways to keep my toddler entertained while I fed the baby:

- *Prepare a children's playlist on the iPod.* All my children have loved listening to story CDs (audio books). The iPod made organising this even easier. I'd import a number of my toddler's favourite stories and make a playlist. We have a connection from our stereo into which I plugged the iPod. If the stories had an associated book, I could have it ready for them to look at while they listened.

- *Read a story.* As I'd have to sit still for more than 10 seconds, it was the perfect opportunity to enjoy a story together.

- *Tell a story.* As we were not always at home when I needed to feed the baby, I found making up my own story to tell the toddler was a simple way of amusing them that required no preparation. I liked to make the central character of the story the toddler themselves! I even turned the story into a learning opportunity by adding a moral to it—for example, two toddlers having difficulty sharing a toy, but finally working out a solution.

- *Pack a snack box.* I prepared a snack box and water bottle for my toddler and preschooler as part of my daily school lunchbox routine. We walked to school each morning and when we returned the baby generally needed to be fed. My toddler could access their snack box and independently have their morning tea at the same time as the baby.

- *Play verbal games.* There were a number of verbal games I'd play with the toddler. The bonus of these games was they could be played anywhere and didn't require any preparation.

  — *'I Spy'.* We played a modified version — for example, 'I spy something red in this room'.

  — *Singing nursery rhymes.* We would sing nursery rhymes requiring participation — for example, saying the animals in 'Old MacDonald Had a Farm'.

  — *Word-association game.* I'd say one word and ask the toddler to say what they thought of — for example, if I said 'big' they might say 'small'; I'd say 'yellow' and they might say 'blue'.

Your support network

Earlier in this chapter I wrote about building up credits with family and friends before baby is born so that, like me, you may feel more comfortable asking for help later on. People do genuinely want to help, but sometimes they're not sure of the best way of assisting you.

Don't be too proud to take help. Too many people make their new parenting experience so much more stressful than it need be by trying to be superwomen and cope alone. It's not natural — humans have always raised infants in groups — and it's so difficult if you have no network of support, community and communication.

Kathryn Sinclair, mum of three

Helping out with the school kids

Transferring babies from car to cot or cot to car often, and the constant running around with a newborn, is not ideal for baby and is also pretty tiring for Mum. With my last two babies I was lucky enough to have great friends who brought my kids home from school on particular nights of the week. This made such a difference to my days and to how frazzled I'd feel at the end of them.

If someone offers to drop your kids home for you, take them up on it! If you have other school families close by, try organising mutually beneficial arrangements with them. For example, you could help them out in some way before baby comes (build up credits) and they can help you out after baby is born. Or, you can arrange to alternate the days that each parent does the pick-up from school. I find people are incredibly generous. Most people won't even expect you to do anything for them and are more than happy to help out. They just may not think or know about offering assistance.

Writing a public 'to-do' list

I love lists and can have many different ones going at any time—for example, one for the blog, one for daily life and one for jobs I want my husband to do. I wouldn't necessarily want everyone to see these lists; they just might reveal too many of my idiosyncrasies! However, whenever I had a newborn I did find it invaluable to have a separate list of tasks I wanted to complete around the house that I was happy for others to see. This list was filled with very simple things such as:

- clean the windows
- mop the floors
- mend the boys' jeans

- hand wash the woollens

- fold the washing.

I had a spot near our kitchen where I kept this list, and it served two purposes: it reminded me of what I needed to do, and it let others know how they could help.

'Things to do' lists — I love them! We all know that we get baby brain and easily forget things, so for me everything goes on a list, even the simple things like returning phone calls. The best part is crossing things off the list, which is a big achievement when you have a newborn.

Sheena Hickman, mum of two

This didn't mean I waved the list in front of every visitor I had in the house. I could never do that! It was meant for those wonderful family members and close friends who popped in to visit us and see the baby, but wanted to help us out too. If I was breastfeeding the baby and they asked me what they could do to help, I could tell them where my 'to do' list was and they could decide for themselves whether they were up for any of those tasks. The list also had the added bonus of letting my husband know which tasks were important to me.

Having your partner at home

It took me until baby number three to work out the 'right' time for my husband to take time off work to help with the new baby. My mum lives in the country so she came and stayed with us for a couple of weeks each time one of our children was born. After baby number two I realised there's no point having two extra adults in the house. For subsequent babies, my husband took a couple of days off around the birth time, then went back to work and took a longer leave period later in the year.

Learn to say 'no' to some visitors in the first couple of weeks (this may be something your husband has to enforce or a sign on the door asking people to come back another time). This is a really special time for both Mum and Dad as usually Dad has taken some precious time off work to spend with you both and it's important to connect as a new family first.

Simone Anderson, mum of one

My experience has been that the toughest part of the first year with a baby is the period from four to six months. By the four-month mark, the effect of continuous broken and limited sleep starts to take its toll on me. The natural adrenalin that you have after the birth of the baby has also worn off. Combine this with the baby's day catnapping starting to kick in and I found this was when I really needed extra support.

For the last three babies, my husband had two weeks off somewhere between the four- to six-month mark and it was fantastic. I could take time to rest more and recharge myself, and the baby didn't have to get dragged around so much either!

Sleep (or lack thereof)

Before kids, I totally took sleep for granted. Once I had my babies it became as precious as gold. And I'll declare that I consider myself pretty lucky as far as the sleep factor goes. Our youngest took the longest to start 'sleeping through' (about eight months).

However, the definition of 'sleeping through' varies from parent to parent. 'Sleeping through', according to our youngest, meant that baby was asleep at 7 pm and woke at 5 am for his first breastfeed of the day. To some parents, 5 am is still the middle of the night. As hard as I tried, he wouldn't go back to sleep even after a breastfeed at that time of the day. He continued to wake at 5 am until he was 18 months old. This is a very early start for parents, especially if you don't go to bed until after 10.30 pm. Babies teach you all sorts of wonderful things, such as coping with sleep deprivation!

I read somewhere: 'don't stand if you can sit, don't sit if you can lie down'. I agree wholeheartedly, particularly the lying down bit!

Lou Woods, mum of four

Coping with sleep deprivation

Get up!

There were days after the birth of our youngest child when I was very tired at 5 am when he woke me up. I'd bring him into bed with me, feed him and then lie there willing him back to sleep. It never worked. He'd crawl all over me, pull my hair, bang books about and find things to pull apart. Before I knew it, another child would join us in bed and the play would get rowdier. My patience would then start to fray and I'd get up in a huff, feeling resentful that I couldn't get more sleep. Compare this to the days when I'd get up with bubs at 5 am, feed him and then just start my day. Yes, I was still tired, but my patience wasn't already shot by 6 am.

Exercise

I know you're thinking, 'How can I exercise when I'm exhausted?' The physical and mental effect of exercising can actually help you feel less tired. Through exercise your body produces those wonderful hormones called endorphins. Endorphins are nature's way of making you feel energised. For me the best by-product of exercise is the improvement in my mood. My

Coping with sleep deprivation (*cont'd*)

local gym opens at 6 am, so after letting my husband sleep until then, being able to hand the baby over and head out to the gym for an hour did wonders to make me feel better. Just imagine, an hour to myself: no questions to answer, no noses to wipe, no fights to break up—heaven!

Watch your intake

Caffeine is quite often the best friend of sleep-deprived parents. However, I've learned the hard way that when you're sleep deprived, rather than caffeine, your body needs more water, and fresh fruit and vegetables. By all means, drink coffee or—like me—your favourite diet cola for a boost, but make sure you drink plenty of water in between and have a healthy diet.

Tag team

Although I was the one who had to breastfeed the baby when he woke at 5 am every morning, one day on the weekend, when sporting commitments allowed, I'd hand our darling baby over to my husband after feeding. He'd then start his day at 5.20 am and I'd go back to sleep for a couple of hours. The other day of the weekend I'd let my husband sleep in. As we were both running on inadequate sleep, taking a tag-team approach meant we both got some more sleep, and neither parent felt animosity towards the other because we both had a turn to sleep in.

Fresh air

On days when my head felt particularly groggy and I wasn't sure I could keep my eyes open for the entire day, I'd find time to get outside with the kids and take in some fresh air. It could be as simple as playing ball games in the backyard with them, or taking a walk to a park for a complete change of environment. Both made me feel better and I found it much easier to cope with the kids outside.

Even super mums need sleep. Sleep deprivation is a killer —sometimes all you need is a power nap to get you through the day, especially the witching hours! The housework will always be there, and most mums know how hard it is to keep on top of everything and won't judge you on how clean the house is.

Sheena Hickman, mum of two

Coping with a baby who catnaps

With the exception of our first child, once each of our babies reached four months of age, their daytime sleeps turned into catnaps. By catnap I mean they would sleep for somewhere between 30 and 45 minutes. Catnapping is generally defined as short bursts of sleep of no more than an hour (that is, one cycle of light and deep sleep). As my experience with catnapping babies grew, I implemented a few strategies for helping myself cope with a baby who's awake a lot during the day.

Accepting that baby is a catnapper

The first time I was faced with dealing with a catnapper (our second child) I was convinced I could get him back to sleep. However, no matter how much I tried it didn't happen, and it really just left me feeling exhausted and frustrated. After that, whenever I started to see the signs that any of our babies' day sleeps were reducing to catnapping, I accepted that for the next couple of months they might not sleep consistently during the day.

I decided not to spend hours trying to get our babies to go back to sleep. I'd try patting them for a short time to determine whether or not they might go back to sleep. If that didn't work, I'd get them up and move on.

Coping with a baby who catnaps (*cont'd*)

Preparing for baby's sleep time

If I needed to complete a task that was difficult to do with baby around, I'd try to prepare everything while baby was still awake. For example, I'd set up everything I needed for cooking dinner—such as getting out the ingredients, stockpot and frying pan—while baby was up. I can generally cook our family meal in 30 to 45 minutes, so once baby had fallen asleep, I'd quickly get to cooking.

Using a baby sling/carrier

Often, our youngest was still very tired after his quick 30-minute catnap, but he liked being placed in a baby carrier. I'd go about my business (vacuuming, doing the washing, and so on) with him in it and quite often he'd take another short nap. This really helped with the feed-play-sleep cycle as he'd then feed better next time around after having had more sleep. It also meant I had two free hands!

Getting out and about

With our youngest, I'd come home after the school drop-off, put him in his cot and see what happened. If he had a catnap and then wouldn't go back to sleep, I'd use this time to go out and run errands. Days could seem very long with a wakeful baby if I didn't break them up with outings.

Stopping to enjoy baby

It's easy to want to work through the day and to view the catnapping habit as a negative interruption. Instead, I tried to take time out to sit on the floor and play with my babies when they were awake, rather than wishing they would have longer sleeps. Playing can be a great way to enjoy your baby and recharge.

Accepting that this is what some babies do

Babies' sleeping patterns are sometimes treated like a competitive sport among mothers, and it's easy to become obsessed with this—as I did with my second child. With my subsequent children I reminded myself that routines are more important to mums than babies in their first year of life. As long as baby is happy and I'm happy, all is okay. And it was always helpful to tell myself, 'This too will pass!'

Taking action

Before baby is born:

- Create your 'essential items' lists for baby and Mum and purchase everything you'll need.

- Spend time gently preparing your other children for the new arrival. Use practical moments (such as when you're washing baby clothes with the kids), books and play so they understand the changes that will happen to their world.

- Work on increasing your kids' independence skills. Make sure they're doing simple tasks they're capable of.

- If you need to change your kids' routines significantly, give them plenty of time to become accustomed to them before baby arrives.

- Build up credits with friends and family so you feel more comfortable asking for help when baby is born.

- When people ask what you would like as a gift for baby, don't be afraid to suggest practical gifts that will make your life easier.

- Create a simple bulk-cooking schedule that fits into your weekly routine so you can build up a stash of meals.

- Create a month of menu plans ready to go once baby is born.

- Stock up on essential items so you're not making continuous trips to the shops with your newborn.

- Purchase or make a small gift for each child on behalf of their new sibling to ease the transition.

We had to re-establish our routine now, as my toddler was struggling with the change in our household routine since his baby brother was brought home six months ago. We made a few tweaks and are now slowly getting back to our routine, which has made a HUGE difference to my toddler's behaviour.

Gill Harrison, mum of two
<www.alicebecomes.blogspot.com>

When baby arrives:

- Find some key strategies that will help get you through the newborn period.

- Prepare in advance simple ways of keeping your toddler entertained while you're feeding baby.

- Don't be afraid to tell people what they can do to help when they ask—they do genuinely want to help you.

To help cope with the effects of baby's sleep patterns on you and your family:

- Don't expect too much of your baby—it can decrease your enjoyment of your precious bundle.

- Exercise and eat well: taking care of yourself is one of the best things you can do for your family.

- If you have a catnapping baby, decide whether you'll accept this or try to change it. Don't let sleep cycles take over your life.

- Share the workload with your partner and make sure you get to sleep in occasionally.

Chapter 5

Tactics for toddlers

I define the toddler years as the period from ages one to three. The toddler years can be such a gorgeous time. Over this period I have the opportunity to watch my child's personality develop, and to see them making sense of their place in the family and further exploring the world around them. As toddlers acquire new skills and practise existing ones, they need support, encouragement and boundaries.

Toddlerhood is the time when I've found I need to begin disciplining my kids. The word discipline has such a negative connotation to many parents. They automatically equate discipline with punishment. I prefer to see discipline in the light of its literal meaning. The word discipline comes from the Latin word *disciplina*, meaning 'instruction' or 'knowledge'. Discipline is about giving the kids knowledge about the social norms of acceptable behaviour and instructing them when they deviate from this.

As a parent I've found it beneficial to spend time with my husband planning how we intend to discipline our kids. The first of these discussions was when our eldest son had just turned one. It was the time of year where all the babies in our playgroup were having their first birthday parties. Our son was a very placid child, but he was going through a stage of exploring the consequences of hitting other kids on the head with random objects. The bigger the reaction, the more he was encouraged to give it another go.

As you can imagine, this was a dangerous stage our toddler was going through—and also pretty embarrassing for me. It's dreadful to see other babies being moved to safety, away from your child. I didn't know how to handle his behaviour. Naturally, I'd physically hold him back from doing it—if I saw what was going on—but in terms of a preventive disciplinary strategy, I was lost. This was when my reading of parenting books started. I wanted to be prepared for the new stages my toddler was going through by researching strategies that would help us discipline him.

Never underestimate the power of using eye contact and dropping to a toddler's physical level to communicate. Teaching them the respect of acknowledgement and using their eyes to communicate starts with their involvement with you.

Jane Vanden Boom, mum of three

Defining your discipline style

Parenting is a confidence game. My husband and I needed more knowledge so we could increase our confidence and be prepared to try new strategies with our toddler. Not everything we tried worked in guiding his behaviour. Some strategies might have worked in the short term, but they didn't sit comfortably with us. Through this process of elimination we began to define our parenting style. By agreeing on some core principles as to how we would discipline our toddler, we were able to give him consistent discipline, which is critical to kids being able to understand the boundaries. We created an approach to parenting that we could easily translate across to new issues (because toddlers always find ways to test their parents!).

Spending time with my husband planning how we intend to discipline our kids is one of the most effective parenting tools we have. Your parenting style will be different from ours, but here are some questions you might like to consider when defining your parenting style:

- Will you set clear boundaries for your children and be consistent in enforcing them?

- Will you smack your children? (Aggression never solves problems in the long term.)

- Will you use reward charts or try getting the children to be self-motivated?

- Will you use time out or bring them in close when your children lose control?

- Will you expect your children to say sorry as an automatic response, even if they're not emotionally connected to it?

- Will you use shouting as a way to get your children's attention?

- Will you apologise when, as the parent, you get it wrong?

- Will you hold a grudge or move on quickly?

- Will you be solution-focused or be focused on finding the culprit?

- Will you try to understand—but not excuse—your children's behaviour?

- Will you provide positive encouragement?

I have children with special needs and using the 'bringing them in close' strategy works especially well when they need help calming down.

Kelly Burstow, mum of four <www.beafunmum.com>

Case study of a two and a half year old toddler

Each of our children reached the 'difficult' toddler stage at the age of two and a half. A fantastic maternal and child health nurse I had for my first two children used to speak about periods of equilibrium and disequilibrium in children.

Disequilibrium refers to the half-year period before a child's birthday (in this instance from two and a half to three years of age) when children can be easily confused, emotional and temperamental, and may have difficulty completing tasks they previously accomplished effortlessly. They then move to a phase of equilibrium over the next half year where they seem to have it all together. I think knowing this information makes the periods of disequilibrium easier to cope with as you know there's an end in sight!

Characteristics of a two and a half year old toddler

Two and a half years is the peak age of disequilibrium. I've experienced four two and a half year olds and it's amazing that even though they all had different personalities, they still exhibited very similar traits at this stage of their lives—for example, they all became:

- *indecisive.* There were times when they seemed to be completely incapable of making a decision if faced with too many choices. Or they would decide they wanted a

Vegemite sandwich only to change their minds when I served it up.

- *fussy.* While toddlers always like to have routines, at this stage of their development mine became very specific about the finer details. For example, they would only eat their breakfast using the 'shiny' spoon, or dry themselves with the purple towel.

- *impossible to satisfy.* No matter how long we stayed somewhere—at the park, a friend's house or the swimming pool, for example—and although I'd give them fair warning that it was time to leave, they always wanted to stay longer.

- *'me'-focused.* They were the biggest thing in their world, and they saw only their own needs. They also overestimated their abilities and would insist that 'me do' everything, even when a task was completely out of their ability range.

- *erratic.* Their emotions were extreme on either side of the pendulum. They were easily excitable and could get wound up very quickly. On the flip side, small things such as peeling the banana skin the wrong way could cause a tsunami-sized meltdown.

Getting your toddler's cooperation

Trying to gain the cooperation of a two year old can sometimes be quite a challenge. Experience with my own children has taught me that I need to be prepared and flexible in how I approach each situation. Here are some strategies for gaining the cooperation of your charming toddler.

Getting your toddler's cooperation (*cont'd*)

Remove temptation

I've things set up so the children can roam freely, but respectfully, around the house. I've removed any major temptations so I don't have to nag all the time. For example, we've moved our eldest child's iPod dock to higher ground. Our toddler just couldn't keep away from its bright lights, and removing it ensures it won't be accidentally broken.

Repeat the request

This is the strategy I use the most when trying to extract a stubborn toddler from the car. Why is it that toddlers never want to get in the car, yet they never want to get out of the car either? We have a people mover, so there's plenty of room for a toddler to run around away from me. Our fourth child loved it when I attempted to grab him: he'd run off the other way, squealing with laughter. I eventually learned not to enter his game. I'd wait at the door of the car and ask him to hop out. If he didn't respond, I'd repeat the request calmly (again and again and again *and* sometimes again), at spaced intervals. Eventually he'd get out of the car by himself.

This is not a quick solution, so it can't be used in every situation. However, I do prefer it, when I have the time, rather than picking up a toddler against their will and tolerating all the associated screaming and crying.

Offer a distraction

This strategy can be hit-and-miss depending on the single-mindedness of the toddler, but it's always worth a try. If I need my current toddler to stop touching something or to move away from an area, I try to create interest in something else that I think will appeal to him in the hope this will make him forget what he was doing.

Show and tell

When attempting to get my toddler to cooperate, I try to make him understand what it is I want of him. Sometimes words aren't enough, and I have to find a way of showing him what I mean. For example, if he asks for a banana just before dinner, I'll pick him up, show him dinner's almost ready and explain that he has to wait until dinner's ready for something to eat.

Listen to your toddler

By taking the time to listen to my toddler, look at him and work out what he's trying to communicate to me, I'm able to make sure I understand what he wants. This prevents meltdowns, which can occur if I misunderstand him and do the wrong thing. When I really listen to him, I can better determine the best way to handle his behaviour.

Have a routine

As you would have noticed by now, I encourage routines for all kids, but they're particularly important for a toddler experiencing disequilibrium. Routines make it easier to gain a toddler's cooperation. They know, for example, that there's time for a short play after lunch and then it's time for their afternoon nap—and that this is not the time for watching TV or running around outside.

Choose your battles carefully

By choosing to focus on the big issues, rather than commenting on every aspect of your toddler's behaviour, you'll find that they're more likely to listen and cooperate. If you monitor their behaviour all day long, they may end up ignoring you because your voice becomes part of the background noise.

My daughter has a very eclectic sense of style and has been independently dressing herself since she was two. This initially caused me a great deal of angst because the combinations

Getting your toddler's cooperation (*cont'd*)

of clothes she would put on were often far from what I would have liked her to be wearing. I'd try to get her to change her clothes, but this would end up in a battle.

When we were out in public and she was wearing one of her more unusual outfits, I'd make comments to other mums along the lines of, 'You can tell she dressed herself this morning'. One day a mum responded to this in a light-hearted manner, saying, 'Your daughter seems very happy with what she's wearing; it seems that Mum is the one with a problem'. And this was indeed true. She had beautiful clothes (lots of generous donations of gorgeous hand-me-downs) and I wanted her to dress a certain way. As awful as this is to admit, I was worried about what other mums might think of the way she was dressed. I was seeing her dress sense as more a reflection of me than as my child having a chance to dress herself how she wanted.

After realising this, I took the next opportunity (when she wasn't home) to reorganise her wardrobe and drawers. I removed all the items that I found particularly difficult to live with and decided from that point on not to comment on her outfits (other than to make sure they were weather-appropriate).

Once I'd accepted that the most important thing was that she dressed herself, her choice of clothes no longer created a battle. There are still moments when she enters the kitchen dressed for the day and behind my smile I cringe a little at the red shorts, purple singlet and long, pink-striped socks. However, I remind myself that she's happy and dressed appropriately for the weather, and that's really all that matters.

Make it fun

By adding some fun to mundane tasks, it's often easier to get a toddler to do what they're supposed to do. Playing peek-a-boo as you dress them, or pretending you don't know where things belong when you're tidying up can make these tasks a bit of fun for you and your toddler.

Spend time with your toddler

On those days when I've had lots of running around to do, there's generally a significant drop in cooperation from our toddler. Stopping for a short burst of time (15 minutes) to sit with him and do something he wants makes him far more likely to cooperate when I ask him to do something. It's important that he feels some of his needs have been met during my busy days as well.

Allow for limited choice

As adults we like to have control over what's going on in our lives and we find it disempowering if choices are taken away from us. Toddlers are just the same. Allowing them a limited choice is helpful in gaining their cooperation. It can be as simple as, 'Do you want Dad or Mum to read the bedtime story?' The choice is not about whether or not the toddler wants to go to bed (because they have to!) but about a discrete part of the going-to-bed process.

I had a free-spirited child who liked to dress herself from an early age. I made a rule for her drawers. She could only go to the top drawers when it was hot and the [lower] drawers were for winter or cold weather.

Tiffany Tregenza, mum of seven

Time management is the single most important skill required when you work from home with a toddler. This doesn't sound very exciting, but if you plan your day correctly, you should be able to enjoy your toddler as well as get some quality work time. If possible make sure you have a shower before your partner leaves for work and get stuck straight into house chores before your toddler goes to sleep. When your toddler is sleeping concentrate solely on your work, ignore the housework/dinner preparations/shopping you haven't completed.

Simone Anderson, mum of one

Teaching independence skills

Independence skills are the daily life and self-care tasks children acquire that allow them to do things for themselves. The acquisition of these skills is not just helpful to parents —as there's one less task for them to do—but they're also critical to building children's self-esteem. Our kids need to be encouraged from a young age to try new things and to know it's okay to make mistakes. Just as toddlers fall many times before they learn to walk, it also takes time for them to learn new skills.

Toddlers will pick up some independence skills—such as walking—by themselves. However, other skills can only be learned with your help and support. Being aware of which skills are appropriate to teach at what age can be useful towards ensuring your toddler is successful in learning each new skill without too much frustration.

Toddler independence skills list

Table 5.1 lists age-appropriate independence skills for toddlers. The skills and associated ages in the table are only examples: if your toddler isn't able to perform the skills at the ages shown, it doesn't mean there's a problem. To use the walking analogy: some kids learn when they're nine months old; others learn when they're 18 months old.

Table 5.1 is not a complete list, but it covers the major skills for the toddler age groups.

Table 5.1: independence skills for toddlers

Age	Skill
1–2 years old	✳ Drink from a small glass
	✳ Feed themselves
	✳ Climb into a chair, turn and sit
	✳ Choose toys from a shelf to play with
	✳ Walk where possible, as opposed to being carried
	✳ Take off shoes, socks and hat
	✳ Wash their face in the bath
	✳ Put rubbish in the bin
2–3 years old	✳ Use a small cloth to wipe up their own spills
	✳ Return toys to their right places
	✳ Put socks and shoes on (no laces)
	✳ Take dirty clothes to laundry basket
	✳ Unscrew lids
	✳ Turn individual pages in a book
	✳ Stand on a safety step to wash own hands
	✳ Be toilet trained or show an interest in toilet training
	✳ Brush or comb their hair

Routines for toddlers

No two toddlers have the same routine, but as a parent I often like to look at other toddlers' routines to see whether I can pick up ideas and inspiration.

Daily routine

It's with this inspiration and the ideas I picked up that I share my daily routine for a toddler with you in table 5.2. This is what a typical day looked like when my youngest child was 22 months old. Naturally, this wasn't followed to exact times each day (for all sorts of reasons), but it's the basic structure we used when caring for our baby.

I have been rising earlier with my twin toddler boys. Surprisingly, I am enjoying being more organised and on top of things earlier. I am now less rushed to get to playgroup and when I am running errands.

Trish, mum of three
<www.mylittledrummerboys.blogspot.com>

Weekly routine

Each school term I put together a children's timetable for the school kids and the preschooler. When I'm doing this, I also write up a simple timetable for our toddler. I don't stick rigidly to this, but it reminds me of the age-appropriate activities I can do with him. Sometimes my days just flash by. Go to the toddler activity prompter table at <www.planningwithkids.com/resources> for ideas of simple activities that will exercise your toddler's gross motor skills.

Table 5.2: daily routine for a toddler

Time	Activity
6.00 am–6.30 am	Wake up! (He's finally moved past waking up at 5.00 am!)
	Breakfast
6.30 am–8.10 am	Get dressed (I dress him) and play
8.10 am–9.15 am	Morning school run with Mum and the big kids
9.15 am–9.30 am	Morning tea
9.30 am–11.30 am	Play
	'Help' Mum with housework (washing, vacuuming, tidying, dusting and cooking)
11.30 am–12.00 pm	Lunch
12.00 pm–12.30 pm	Story and song
12.30 pm–2.30 pm	Sleep
2.30 pm–3.00 pm	Wake up (If I'm lucky, he will sleep for two hours; some days it's less.)
	He's quite clingy when he wakes up, so he'll spend at least 15 minutes sitting on my lap or glued to my hip before venturing off to play.
3.00 pm–3.30 pm	Afternoon school run to pick up the big kids
3.30 pm–5.00 pm	Afternoon tea
	Play with the big kids
5.00 pm–5.30 pm	Tiredness kicks in
	Stay with Mum and 'help' prepare and serve dinner
5.30 pm–6.00 pm	Dinner
6.00 pm–6.30 pm	Bath and play
6.30 pm–7.00 pm	Story, song and breastfeed
7.00 pm	Sleep

A toddler-friendly everyday bag

Most parents with young kids have an everyday bag: it's the one thing we can't leave the house without. As babies become toddlers I've had to add things to the bag that will keep the toddler (and the older children) entertained should we get held up, or if we're at an adult-focused event. Besides the essential items—nappies, nappy wipes and a change of clothes—there are some stock items listed in table 5.3 that I like to have in the bag and replenish on a regular basis. They make being out with a toddler so much easier.

Table 5.3: everyday bag contents

Item	Use
Tissues	I use a combination of travel packs and great big handfuls from the box at home. You can never have too many.
Bandaids	The healing power of a bandaid is truly amazing!
Pencils and paper	I pack a small pencil case, complete with pencils, rubber, pencil sharpener and homemade recycled note pads.
Cards	I have a Playschool pack of cards in my bag so I can play 'Memory' with my toddler and preschooler. It helps pass the time waiting for the big kids.
Hair ties	These are handy to have stashed in the bag for me and/or my daughter. They can also double as a rubber band if I need to try to keep something together.
Matchbox cars	Toddlers love little cars so I like to have some in the bag to use in emergencies for entertainment or distraction purposes.
Old shopping bags	I have a couple knotted and slipped into a side pocket. They're useful for many different things including putting dirty/wet clothes in and for rubbish if we're in a park that has a 'carry in carry out' policy.

Item	Use
Sunscreen	Essential for my fair-skinned babes—I keep a small tube (contained within a zip-lock bag, in case of leakage) in a pocket of the bag.
Coins	After too many experiences of not having change for parking meters, I now stash away some coins in a small coin purse.
Safety pin	A very simple but helpful tool in many situations. I've used it to hold together a dress strap (my own actually) and to rethread and hold together broken elastic in shorts.
Dice	Two or three dice are great for playing quick number games.
Antibacterial hand gel	A small tube of this means I can clean my hands after nappy changes etc., even if there's no water on hand.

Taking action

- Take the time to talk to your partner and discuss your discipline style.

- Be prepared for your toddler to swing between periods of calm (equilibrium) and chaos (disequilibrium).

- Develop strategies for gaining cooperation from your toddler that will help avoid toddler meltdowns.

- Decide which battles you'll take on with your toddler.

- Spend time teaching your toddler life skills to increase their independence and self-esteem.

- Establish a routine for your toddler's daily activities.

- Create a toddler timetable to act as a prompt for activities you can play with them.

Chapter 6

Preparation for preschoolers

The terms 'preschool' and 'kindergarten' have different meanings depending on which state you live in. In Victoria, children can do two years of preschool education before they enter school. These years are generally referred to as three-year-old and four-year-old kindergarten. This chapter is about this lovely stage in a child's life, where they've turned three or four but are yet to start primary school.

Preparing for the kinder years

As I've had several children and have seen the speed with which they head off to school, I've learned to cherish the remaining years before they venture into formal education. So, when I start preparing them for preschool, I don't drill them with flash cards or teach them to read. I ensure they have the social, independence and organisational skills that will make their transition to preschool easier for them and me.

I made sure we purchased our kindergarten 'uniform' (a T-shirt with the kinder logo on it) at the AGM the year previous to him starting kinder.

Bree Whitford, mum of two

Social skills

Kids need to be able to socialise and interact successfully with their kinder classmates. Social skills are the learnt behaviours that allow us to interact and communicate with others. As adults we do these things automatically and it can be easy to forget these skills need to be learned. Throughout our daily interactions with our preschooler, my husband and I role model and encourage social skills such as:

- *listening to an adult other than Mum or Dad.* In group settings such as parties, we let other adults ask our preschooler to do things.

- *asking politely for what they want.* When we're visiting friends and he's thirsty, we encourage our preschooler to ask the adult of the house for a drink—using his best manners, of course!—rather than getting it for him.

- *understanding rules and boundaries.* When visiting places that have signs explaining rules, we take the time to point them out and read them to him, for example, 'You're not allowed to put your feet on the seats on trains'.

- *expressing their feelings.* I try to label my own emotions when talking to my kids. When they react, I also try to reflect in words how they're reacting. This helps them build an emotional vocabulary so they can express how they feel. Almost all my kids at some point have told me they are 'very frustrated' or 'cross' with me—phrases I've used many times myself about them!

- *sharing toys and equipment.* Even with several children, I still have to work with the younger kids to ensure they share with other children. Sharing can be hard at times for kids, so I try to talk to them about empathy: how would they feel if they weren't allowed to play with that toy?

- *taking turns.* Board games are fantastic for getting young kids to practise taking turns. While it's sometimes hard to watch how a youngster reacts to losing, I've found it's really important not to always let them win. At preschool they have to accept taking turns and losing so it's good for them to learn how to cope with this.

- *problem solving and compromising.* Allow younger kids to work out solutions to everyday problems that occur at home. For example: there are only three mangoes left, but four kids want mango for dessert. By asking questions, you can help your preschooler arrive at a solution. You may have to guide them initially to help them realise they may have to compromise to reach a solution.

I try to keep in the back of my mind that although I teach my children the importance of sharing, it is equally as important for children to have special items that they don't have to share—their own precious treasures that are just their own.

Cassandra Circosta, mum of two

Independence skills

As with a toddler, you also have to plan time for teaching a preschooler age-appropriate skills. A great tip I learned from my eldest son's Montessori teacher was when teaching children new skills, don't bombard them with too much information. Show them the activity first, without words, allowing them to take in the steps. Too much talk can distract them from observing how to do it. You may have to repeat the task. Then it's their turn. Allow them to do it on their own. Let them self-correct where possible and give them time to work out any problems that arise.

With my first child, I found it easy to fall into the trap of doing things for him that he was capable of doing himself. It's great to have a list of 'life skills' like in table 6.1 for each stage of the preschool years as a reminder about what they should be accomplishing.

Table 6.1: independence skills for preschoolers

Age	Skill
3–4 years old	* Use the toilet independently
	* Wash their own hands
	* Brush their teeth (although dentists recommend that parents brush once a day until children are nine years old)
	* Choose their own clothes and dress themselves
	* Tidy up after themselves: spills, mess, toys
	* Blow their own nose and cover up when they cough
	* Clean themselves in the bath
	* Pour themselves a drink
	* Pack and carry their own bag
4–5 years old	* Follow simple two-step directions
	* Follow rules of games (mostly!)
	* Know their full name
	* Fasten and undo simple buttons and zippers
	* Carry own meal to the table
	* Cut with scissors
	* Ride a tricycle

The table highlights a selection of age-appropriate independence skills for preschoolers, but it's not an exhaustive list of what preschoolers are capable of. The time taken to master these skills will differ among preschoolers. Kids have varying patterns of development, and if you have any concerns about your child's abilities you should consult a medical professional.

> We encouraged independence with hair grooming by playing hairdressers on the weekends. When your child is ready to take the brush reins solo, ignore the imperfections and remind yourself, 'Life is not a fashion parade'.
>
> Jane Vanden Boom, mum of three

Organisational skills

In our family the preschooler not only needs to become independent for his own self-confidence, but also to help make sure we leave the house on time during the school week. Our preschoolers have needed help with learning how to organise themselves. There are two key ways we've helped them.

Organising clothes

To help our preschooler with the job of getting himself dressed, I've organised his clothes in a way that he can access them easily.

- *Drawers.* Our preschooler has two very large drawers. He used to make a mess of the drawers when looking for something to wear. To solve this problem I placed shoeboxes and cut-up nappy boxes in his drawers. These boxes created separate, defined areas for each type of clothing item. There are areas for socks, underwear and pyjamas in the top drawer. In the bottom drawer, there are separate sections for tops and shorts. Now he can easily find what he's looking for, and he can also put his own clothes away in their right places.

- *Wardrobes.* The wardrobes in the younger kids' room have low-hanging rails, which make it easy for the kids to select clothes to wear, and to put them away. The ideal situation would be adjustable rails so you could move them as the kids grow. If you have standard floor-to-ceiling wardrobes, try placing a non-slip stool in the bottom of the wardrobe. This allows preschoolers independent access to their clothes.

- *Minimising the number of clothes.* My preschooler often gets to the stage where he has too many clothes in his wardrobe and drawers. He's fourth in line, so he gets clothes passed down from his older siblings. We've also received some great hand-me-downs from friends who have older children. All of this can result in cluttered drawers and wardrobes, making the task of choosing clothes difficult for him.

I routinely go through his drawers, removing any clothes that no longer fit him and anything that's become shabby. However, sometimes that's not enough. For example, last winter he somehow accumulated five pairs of pyjamas, which was simply too many. It's taken me about 10 years to work out that when it comes to clothes for a preschooler less is definitely better. Even if clothing items are in good condition and still fit him, I remove as much as possible to limit his choices and to keep the drawers sparsely filled for easier access.

Creating a visual routine chart

We've always used a routine chart of some sort to help our preschoolers get organised for their day at kinder. For our third son I modified our approach and worked with him to create a visual routine chart. The chart outlined the key activities he had to complete each morning in photographic format.

In the week leading up to the start of kinder, I photographed him one morning enacting each part of the routine he'd be following once kinder started and created a chart with a picture of him doing each of these things under the following headings: breakfast, teeth, dress, sunscreen, hat, morning tea, go!

What I loved the most about this process was how much my preschooler enjoyed it. We had to print out two copies of the chart because he wanted to hold and read his routine over and over again. Being involved in the making of his routine made him feel attached to it, so whenever he needs redirecting in the morning I can use the routine chart to get him back on track.

Find a blank template to make your own routine chart at <www.planningwithkids.com/resources>.

Opportunities for learning

Preschoolers are like sponges. They soak up everything around them. I'm constantly in awe of how much children develop during the preschool years. The beginnings of early literacy and numeracy take hold and kids have a never-ending thirst for knowledge. As a parent I have the opportunity to encourage and foster this learning. My philosophy has always been to 'follow the child' and support their interests.

> *Life with a preschooler is much easier if you can dress up everyday tasks with 'a spoonful of sugar'. Making tasks seem fun will always get the job done.*
>
> Caroline Boult, mum of two

Building learning into your daily routine

With five children, finding the time to fit in learning opportunities can be tricky. Kids learn in such a dynamic way that I've found the easiest way to engage them in learning is to fit it into our daily life. This allows me to stimulate and support our preschooler's interest in early numeracy and literacy regularly. The best part is that it's an enjoyable way to interact and spend time with our preschooler.

Learning while walking

Taking a walk with your preschooler is good both for fitness and for the child's learning. Walking is a lovely, informal way of providing numerous learning opportunities, such as:

- *the letterbox game.* As we walk along we take turns in reading aloud the numbers on the letterboxes of the houses we pass. (Learning opportunity: number recognition.)

- *'I went shopping and I bought ...'.* This is a modified version of the traditional game that I play with the older children. One of us says, 'I went shopping and I bought four things ...', for example, 'I bought an apple, a carrot, juice and bread'. The other player has to remember the four items. (Learning opportunities: memory; counting up to four.)

Learning while waiting

When children reach school age, the after-school activities generally begin. With a bit of planning, the time spent attending after-school activities can provide opportunities for short sessions of fun, such as:

- *'I Spy'.* This is a modified version of the original game. I put three toys in front of us. Each one starts with a different sound—for example, a car, a ball and a snake. I get my preschooler to name all the objects. This clarifies that we have the same name in mind for each object—for example, a ball (not a football). We then discuss the starting sound of each object before starting to play. Then, for example, I say, 'I spy with my little eye, something starting with c', always using the phonetic sound of the starting letter. (Learning opportunity: start awareness of phonetic sounds of the alphabet.)

- *rolling dice.* My kids love dice, and this is a game the older children can play with us. We take turns at rolling two dice and then work out which number each one has rolled. We then work out who won by finding the highest or lowest number. For the older kids I add more dice so they can practise their addition or multiplication. (Learning opportunities: start building one-to-one matching numeracy; understanding the relativity of numbers.)

Learning while helping around the house

These activities can be done as part of your daily home duties.

- *Cooking.* Cooking with a preschooler provides many opportunities for them to learn early numeracy skills. Discussing amounts in numerical terms, time values and number recognition on measuring cups or in a recipe all provide a natural setting for familiarisation with numbers. (Learning opportunity: general numeracy awareness.)

- *Sorting and classifying.* There are many opportunities in the daily activities of home life for a preschooler to practise sorting and classifying skills. Tasks such as putting away the cutlery, sorting the dirty washing into whites and colours, and putting waste in the right bin — rubbish, compost and recyclables — make the preschooler think about which items are the same and which are different. (Learning opportunity: introduction to mathematical vocabulary and concepts.)

When I had my first child I did so many activities with him, and we were out most days. When my second and then third children were born it became too hard to do that many activities and I spent a long time feeling guilty that my second child in particular was missing out. Then I finally realised that he actually preferred staying home to going to different activities and that none of them actually needed to do endless things outside the home.

Jacquie Davidson, mum of three

Learning while shopping

Going shopping isn't always my preschooler's favourite activity. However, engaging him in the shopping process results in less conflict and fewer complaints. This involvement also provides learning opportunities, such as:

- *the gathering game.* When we're at the market or the supermarket, my preschooler is my 'gatherer'. I tell him how many of each item we need and he gathers the right number and puts them in the trolley. (Learning opportunities: practise counting; one-to-one matching.)

- *paying for purchases.* Allowing our preschooler, where possible, to have a turn at paying for the goods we purchase is by far his favourite activity. We talk about the numbers on the money, how there are dollars and cents and whether or not we will get change, which helps him to start understanding how money works. (Learning opportunity: introduction to currency.)

- *spotting symbols.* I try to point out to my preschooler any symbols around the shops or any we can see from the car. We talk about how a symbol is a short way of explaining something. For example, the picture on exit signs of a man running shows where we can exit a building; the crossed-out 'P' symbol on signs in parking areas means you can't park there because it's not allowed and you'll get fined. (Learning opportunity: introduction to symbols.)

Preschoolers and technology

TV became a bit of an issue in our house some years ago when our eldest son was a preschooler. I originally tried restricting his viewing to special occasions only. As a consequence, he'd often ask, 'Is it time to watch some TV now?' He didn't know when he would be allowed to watch TV again, so he took the approach of asking frequently whether he could, just in case I said yes.

My husband and I talked through our existing approach and how we could change it. We decided on a time limit of 30 minutes and made the TV session at the end of the day. That way it was clear to him that TV time was late in the day, and he stopped constantly asking me about it. This also gave me time at the end of the day to breastfeed the baby quietly.

Talking books are a great alternative to TV when having down time in the afternoon. You can get them from the library. My kids loved Winnie-the-Pooh, The Faraway Tree *and even* Bob the Builder.

Georgina Rechner, mum of three

Sharing

As we've had more children and the age between the eldest and youngest has increased, we've had to come up with a roster to ensure everyone has a turn at watching something they like. We developed a roster system to manage the kids' competing needs. As they grew older we also incorporated time on the computer and playing on the Wii into the roster. They're treated the same as TV as they're all sedentary activities and we now refer to this as technology time. The older children have longer technology-time sessions now, as they stay up longer than the younger ones.

The planned TV time has served us very well. The kids have grown accustomed to it and have accepted it. When their show is over, they get up and turn the TV off, and they never go into the lounge room and turn the television on without permission. However, they do get very excited when we hire a new movie as they get to watch a lot more TV than their standard allocation of 30 minutes.

The child whose name (or in this example age) appears next to the day is allowed to choose a technology activity: Wii, computer or TV. If they choose TV, they're also allowed to choose the program they want to watch (within family guidelines). The other children then agree on how they will share the remaining available technology during that time. Due to the spread of ages, it can sometimes be quite challenging for them to find a middle ground. However, as their time is ticking away, they usually come to some form of compromise! The TV roster changes regularly to take into account after-school activities and the kids' ages. We also aim to have one night a week that's technology free.

Table 6.2 (overleaf) shows a typical example of our kids' evening routine for technology usage.

Table 6.2: technology-time roster

Day	Child	Amount of time
Monday	None	0
Tuesday	2 year old	30 minutes
Wednesday	7 year old	30 minutes
Thursday	4 year old	30 minutes
Friday	7 year old	30 minutes
Saturday	9 year old	1 hour
Sunday	12 year old	1 hour

I know a number of families where the kids are not allowed technology time during the week, but they can use technology as much as they want on weekends. I can see how this could work well for some families. Regardless of the routine make-up, it's the actual routine that's critically important. A technology routine ensures kids know when they may use technology, and puts limits on the amount of time spent on technology activities.

While not for everyone, our house works so much better with the 'no TV/no PC' (includes DS' etc.) rule from Monday until Friday afternoon for school kids (any preschoolers had a TV option in the morning after school drop-off). There are no arguments over this rule because it was enforced from day one of school commencing and it removes massive distractions during the week, allowing kids to entertain themselves, do homework and play sports.

Belinda Burr, mum of three

What to watch on TV

A drawback of the roster system and leaving TV time until later in the day is the limited choice of programs as kids' shows are generally shown earlier in the day. Technology, however, actually solves that problem. We talked to the kids about the shows they want to watch and we now record them. The added advantage of recording shows is that the kids can fast forward through the advertisements.

There are a number of fantastic kids' shows on TV that can provide entertainment and education. Some kids' shows can provide inspiration for activities at home and for investigating further learning. For example, the children's television show *Play School* has fantastic resources on its website. Each week it details the themes for the upcoming shows. The program notes take you through the songs, stories and activities they will be performing on each show, and give parents ideas for activities they can share with their children.

Find suggestions on age-appropriate TV shows and their websites at <www.planningwithkids.com/resources>.

What to play online

We use a planned and moderated approach for introducing our kids to the online world. Preschoolers quickly learn to navigate the screens and develop the hand–eye coordination skills to be able to play online computer games. Limited, and used in conjunction with other learning tools, the computer can be a fantastic learning tool. However, finding online games that are age-appropriate and of interest to a preschooler is important in the not-so-regulated online environment. While some games can be fun and free, kids can be exposed to non-stop advertising.

When choosing an online game for your preschooler consider the following factors:

- Does it contain advertising?
- What's the key message of the game?

- Will it help enhance a skill (for example, memory, fine-motor skills, number recognition, colour identification)?

- Is the game built so preschoolers can operate it easily themselves?

A list of age-appropriate online games for preschoolers can be found at <www.planningwithkids.com/resources>.

Taking action

- Role model and give preschoolers opportunities to practise social skills.

- Spend time teaching your preschooler independence skills to help their transition to kinder.

- Organise your preschooler's clothes so they can access them easily.

- Review their clothes regularly, removing items, so your preschooler is not overwhelmed by choice.

- Create a visual routine chart with your preschooler to use as a prompt for getting ready in the mornings.

- Build small learning activities into your daily routine to encourage interest in early literacy and numeracy.

- Decide on a routine for your preschooler's access to technology.

- Investigate which TV shows are most appropriate for your preschooler.

- If they're interested, plan time to teach your preschooler how to navigate a computer.

Chapter 7

Strategies for schoolchildren

Once children reach kinder and school age, your weekday life during the school term begins to run to a schedule that's set by others. For me, a key to both kids and parents enjoying the school year is for it to be as organised as possible and for the organisation to come from the whole family, not just Mum and Dad.

Preparing for school

Readiness for school is a widely discussed topic among parents. I don't believe there's one answer to the question 'At what age should my child start school?' I suggest if you're looking for an answer to this question you should consider the following:

- Each child is different and decisions should be made on the personality and circumstances of each child (what might be good for their best friend, or sister, may not be good for them).

- Take advice from your child's preschool teacher. They will be able to give you invaluable insight into your child's cognitive, social and emotional development.

- Remember that education is not a race.

If you've decided your child is ready for school, prepare them for the experience in a simple, fuss-free way.

- Kids like to know what's coming up, so it's important to let them know when they'll be starting school. Talk casually about school as they begin their transition sessions.

- Ensure they can manage their school clothes. The pull strings on new hats or buckles on shoes may be rigid. Have them practise using these so they can manage them easily at school by themselves.

I always try to have uniforms ready in the evening. I learned to do this after spending many valuable minutes in the morning looking for sock pairs in the clean-laundry basket!

Danielle Spagnol, mum of four

- Make sure they can pack and unpack their school bag and hang it on a hook.

- Check they can open and close their lunchbox and drink bottle.

- Use a calendar to show them the graduated introduction to school as this will help set their expectations. Most schools either have half days or have a day off during the week as they ease children into the school routine.

- In the last week before school, try keeping major activities to a minimum and aim for an early bedtime each night.

- If you're going to walk to school, go for a practice walk a few days beforehand. Show your child where you'll wait for them at the end of the day.

- Read stories about children starting school and discuss any questions your child raises.

Creating a school schedule

When my eldest son went off to school, it took me more than a year to realise that I needed to change my habits so that he'd become more responsible for getting himself organised for school. Using a tip from his classroom teacher, I created a school schedule for him. Tables 7.1 and 7.2 (overleaf) are examples of school schedules that I continue to create with all of our primary school–aged kids.

The aim of the children's schedule is to:

- show them what their weekly activities are

- allow them to take responsibility for having the right gear on the right days

- familiarise early readers with the days of the week and other commonly used words.

Table 7.1: grade one school schedule

Monday	Tuesday	Wednesday	Thursday	Friday
	Fitness	Drama	Sport	Assembly
	Music	Chess	Mandarin	
	Show and share		Library	

Table 7.2: grade one after-school schedule

Monday	Tuesday	Wednesday	Thursday	Friday
Swimming	Reading	Dance	Reading	Reading
Reading		Reading		

School schedules help kids prepare for school independently each morning. They have substantially reduced the morning nag factor at our house. I no longer have to ask, 'Have you got your library book?' or 'Did you choose something for show and share?' I now leave these responsibilities fully with each child.

A school schedule template can be found at <www.planningwithkids.com/resources>.

Coping with school paperwork

There are peak periods—such as the start of the school year—when, without a system in place, I used to feel in a complete mess with all the school paperwork. After missing a couple of important notices, I realised that to stay on top of things I needed to develop a way of coping with the constant influx of slips, forms and newsletters that are very much a part of school life.

Allocating time for paperwork

One of my biggest time wasters with paperwork was handling the same items several times. When the kids brought me their notices after school, I'd read them and decide whether they needed action or not. If they needed action I'd put them aside for later. However, when later came, as I had only skim-read the notices I'd have to read them all over again and then action them.

Now the kids put their notices in a folder on the kitchen bench. I don't worry about them until the kids are in bed. I then read them once and action them straight away.

The school newsletter

Our school newsletter is the main source of information we receive from the school. To help me keep track of all the school events, once I receive it I write all key dates on the calendar, complete the required tear-off slips, then hang the current newsletter on a clip on the fridge for future reference.

Sending back forms

Each child has a communication pouch that they keep in their school bag for the exchange of notices between home and school. In the evenings when I fill in the forms that need to go back to school, I place the completed forms in the kids' lunchboxes for them. The lunchboxes sit open on the kitchen bench each morning for the kids to collect. It's the kids' responsibility to ensure the completed forms make their way into the communication pouch and back to school.

The child information sheet

I picked up this tip from another mother at school, so thanks to Danielle for sharing it with me. There are a series of forms that have to be filled in at the start of the year for each school child—for example, the Neighbourhood Excursion form, which gives the school permission to take the kids on a walk around the block. The forms all require particular details to be filled in, such as the date of the child's last tetanus injection, our Medicare number, and our doctor's name and contact details. This information is also needed for other forms throughout the year (school camp permission forms, for example).

I've compiled a child information sheet (see table 7.3) so I don't have to find the kids' Maternal and Child Health books and all the relevant cards needed to complete these forms. As this information doesn't change very often, I can continue to use it in future years as well.

Table 7.3: child information sheet

Child	1	2	3
Last tetanus			
Medicare no.			
Health insurance			
Doctor's name			
Doctor's address			
Doctor's phone no.			
Allergies			

Organising after-school activities

As each of our children starts going to school, the number of after-school activities we have to juggle increases. If not managed well, the after-school run-around can severely impact on my busyness and that of the little ones.

We have swimming at 5.30 pm, so I usually do a slow cooker meal in winter on those days. Our routine is to have a shower, get into pyjamas and have a snack at the pool, so when we get home around 7 pm dinner is waiting for us and the kids can quickly eat, clean teeth and go to bed. If they fall asleep in the car on the way home we can just lift them straight into bed. In the summer I usually pack a picnic dinner (often zucchini slice and fruit), which we eat at the tables at the pool before coming home and going straight to bed.

Virginia Lindenmayer, mum of three

Juggling after-school activities

The following tips have helped us manage after-school activities more effectively.

No after-school activities for preps in term one

During term one preps are busy adjusting to attending school for long days, five days in a row. Preps are generally very tired in term one, even if they've attended childcare full time in the past. A tired prep means an emotional child, so I find the less for them to do after school, the better. Even if a prep child has to come along to their older siblings' activities, at least they're not having to listen to and follow instructions in a structured environment.

Sharing the driving

Once the kids have settled into their new after-school activities, I've found it incredibly helpful to find another family with whom I can share the drop-offs and pick-ups. For example, I only take my daughter to her dance class once a fortnight. Another lovely mum, Kate, and I alternate bringing the girls home from school and then taking them to and from dancing.

Juggling after-school activities (*cont'd*)

Playing in the park

I've noticed that I take my younger children to play in the park less often than I did the older ones. Training grounds for cricket and football are usually located near a playground so I make the most of these opportunities by playing with the kids at the nearby playgrounds.

Playing games

One of the items I keep in my everyday bag is a pack of cards. If we're attending an after-school activity for one child at an indoor space, it's an opportunity to sit with the younger children and play cards. Pencils and paper or a colouring book are also handy for making the most of our time together.

Limiting the number of activities

Children can often overestimate their energy levels so we limit the number of after-school activities they participate in. Education consultant Kathy Walker recommends only one to two activities for children aged four to eight.

We restrict the number of after-school activities to two per child. With three children who currently participate in after-school activities, this means we can have up to six scheduled events after school. Thankfully, all our children have chosen swimming as one activity and we have them all enrolled on the same day at the same time. Even with this efficiency, some terms we only have one school night per week with no scheduled activity.

Dinner comes first

As the children get older, the after-school activities start later, often around 5.30 or 6.00 pm. By the time they've finished, it's very late for the younger children (aged six and under) to eat dinner. So on the days when we have late finishes I swap afternoon tea with dinner time.

When the children come home from school, they just have a piece of fruit and then I serve their evening meal at around 4.30 pm. I then pack a healthy snack for them to have on the way home from the after-school activities. This change in routine has two advantages: the children actually eat all of their dinner, and I don't have hungry (as well as tired) children waiting at after-school activities.

Having dinner prepared

When I do my menu planning, I make sure I factor in after-school activities. On days when we'll be out and about straight after school, I make sure I prepare something earlier in the day—or a plan for a very quick meal—so we can eat at the usual time.

Completing homework

I encourage our children to do their homework on the nights when they don't have after-school activities. This prevents situations where they're up late finishing homework because we've arrived home late.

Ensuring enjoyment

It's important to stop every so often to check that your children are actually enjoying their after-school activities. We keep it simple for our children: they can choose what they want to do, but if they start an activity they must see it through to the end of the term or season. If they no longer want to do that activity once the season or term has finished, they can stop.

Booking after-school activities early

It's important for us to book or rebook after-school activities as early as possible. For after-school activities such as swimming,

Juggling after-school activities (*cont'd*)

doing so means we have a greater chance of having all our kids in the pool for their lessons at the same time. One swimming time compared with three different ones makes my life much easier.

Get homework done as soon as they arrive home from school: 30 minutes for primary and an hour for secondary is not much to add to the end of their school day.

Stephen Fulton, dad of three

Managing homework

Personally, I'm not an advocate of homework in primary school. There are many reasons for this, and if you're interested in this issue Alfie Kohn has written an excellent book called *The Homework Myth: Why Our Kids Get Too Much of a Bad Thing*. The book outlines current research that explains why homework doesn't produce the educational benefits its supporters claim it does.

However, even with my philosophical opposition to homework we've sent our children to a school that does expect them to complete homework. From grade three, children are expected to complete on average 15 to 30 minutes of homework each evening. From personal experience, I know that homework can become a battleground between children and parents. Having learned the hard way, I can offer some suggestions on how you may like to manage homework in relation to your primary-school children.

Giving children responsibility

For a long time after our eldest child started doing homework, I was really the one wearing the responsibility for it being completed. I'd check at the start of the week what he had to do and then I'd check throughout the week that it was being done. He didn't have to worry about remembering to do his homework because I did that for him. It reached the point where if I didn't remind him it wouldn't be completed.

It took me a while to realise the problem I'd created. For him to become more responsible about his homework, I needed to step back. I met with his teacher and explained that I'd no longer be checking that he'd completed his homework, and that it might take him some time to get into the practice of remembering it himself. I wanted him to understand that if his homework wasn't done there would be direct consequences, such as having to complete it at lunchtime. It was an essential part of the learning process for him to understand the consequences of not doing his homework.

My son was incredibly happy about my decision to back off. He'd resented what I saw as 'checking', which he saw as nagging. There are still times when he doesn't hand in his homework or he remembers it only the morning that it's due. He's had to endure the consequences of this and it's a relief for me not to have to be the enforcer. I still take an active interest in his homework and I help him as needed, but I've learned not to take responsibility for or nag about it.

Deciding how much help to give

I believe it's important to be available to assist my kids with their homework questions and requests. We've set expectations around this assistance. For example, they can't expect me to stop immediately and help when I'm in the middle of cooking dinner or when I'm reading bedtime stories to the younger kids. If they need chunks of my time to help them, they have to organise a suitable time with me.

The best way I can help my kids with their homework is not to focus on the content, but on the logical process they should follow to successfully complete it. For example, when our eldest son was in grade six he had to write a speech to present to the class. Before he started, we sat together and documented the actions he should take:

- write a plan

- write the first draft

- write the second draft

- transfer the speech to hand cards

- practise the speech.

Because of his tendency to leave homework to the last minute, we allocated a date to each of these actions so he could spread the workload over the time he had available. Before he started his plan, we spoke about the key elements of a speech—that is, the beginning, middle and end. What he wrote, how he wrote it, and so on was all left to him. My support was restricted to the process he would follow. As he completes more homework tasks like this one, he becomes more familiar with the process and I can step further away.

Designating a homework area (or not!)

Our eldest son has always completed his homework in a variety of places. Sometimes he'd do it at his desk in his room, sometimes on the floor, occasionally at the dining table and other times in our study. This used to drive me crazy. The first tip you read on getting kids to do their homework is almost always to have a designated area for them to complete it. So, with this in mind, I frequently used to ask him to move back to his desk, which would annoy him.

Then, when he was in grade six, I read an article from *The New York Times*—'Forget what you know about good study habits'—and it made me change my view on having a designated homework area. The article discussed key research findings that showed how changing your study location can actually help improve retention. By making my son move when he was in the middle of his homework, I was interrupting his workflow. My demand also affected his mood towards his homework and it was becoming another source of conflict.

Now I let him complete his homework wherever he wants and he's much happier. Moreover, there's been no decrease in the quality of his homework.

I did find, however, that essential study items such as rulers, pencils, sharpeners and glue would end up strewn across the house. To eliminate this we created a homework corner. This is where we keep all the necessary homework items, including the dictionary and thesaurus. We have a tiered filing tray and each child has their own draw for storing their works in progress and stationery. Regardless of where they complete their homework, they have to return their items to the homework corner.

Where kids feel comfortable completing their homework is driven by their personality. My second son operates very differently from his older brother. He always sits at the dining table and finds it frustrating if I'm using the table and he can't work there. Finding a homework space that suits each child is more important for us than having fixed rules for where homework should be completed.

Making time for homework

When our second son began receiving homework in grade three, the first thing he did was work out how he'd complete it around his after-school activities. He wanted a timetable to follow so he'd know what he had to do each night. I printed out a blank table onto which he could write his homework plan. He fills it in and uses it to manage his homework.

It's worth noting that my eldest son never did anything like this in his entire time at primary school. This level of homework planning doesn't necessarily work for all kids, but if you think it would suit your child, then have a look at table 7.4, or you can find a template for them to complete at <www.planningwithkids.com/resources>.

Table 7.4: grade three homework schedule

Monday	Tuesday	Wednesday	Thursday	Friday
'Look, Say, Cover, Write, Check'	Maths Spelling activity	Cricket training Maths	'Look, Say, Cover, Write, Check'	Reading
Reading	Maths	Reading	Maths	
Swimming	Reading		Reading	

Satisfying those empty tummies

Thirst and hunger can be massive distractions so I make sure my children have had afternoon tea before they start their homework. How quickly the kids get into their homework after school is determined by their individual temperaments. One of my children needs some down time before getting into his homework. Another likes to get into his straight away and have it completed as soon as possible. Allowing each child the flexibility to work in a way that suits them stops many arguments over homework.

I have afternoon tea ready and waiting when the children arrive home from school. It all feels a bit fifties, but they are so much nicer to me when they walk in the door and there is a scrumptious afternoon tea on the table. Sometimes it is home cooked goodies but not always. They refuel, and the afternoon and evening are off to a good start.

Katie McIntosh, mum of eight

Organising the school gear

Both my husband and I love things being in their place. When it comes to our kids, we've worked out that if we want them to put their things away, they need to know exactly where each item has to go.

Over the past couple of years my husband has placed many hooks around our house and we've created designated areas for school gear. The kids know where they have to place their school gear and can easily access their hooks.

School bags

Before we hung bag hooks in the laundry, we used to find the kids' school bags in their bedrooms, at the back door, in the lounge room — or wherever they dropped them when they came home from school. It would drive me crazy walking around the house and almost tripping over a school bag that had been left in the middle of the hallway. The kids now know to hang them on their hooks as soon as they come in from school. Not only does this save me from tripping over them, it also means it's less likely that things will be misplaced if they fall out of their open bags.

I wish I could say that this system means the kids hang their bags up 100 per cent of the time without being asked to.

Unfortunately, that's not the case. The hooks have, however, significantly reduced the number of times I've had to remind them to hang up their bags.

Lunchboxes

Once the kids have hung up their school bags, they know they have to place their lunchboxes on the kitchen bench along with any school notices. Of course, knowing and doing are two separate things. On the days when the kids don't place their lunchboxes on the bench, I leave their school lunches on the bench. It's up to them to find their lunchboxes and pack them.

School shoes

Just like me, our kids love not wearing shoes. Before entering the house after school most of them take off their shoes. This used to lead to the frustrating situation of having six or more pairs of shoes scattered at our back door. My husband's creativity and resourcefulness once again came to the rescue. He altered a bookshelf to fit flat against a wall near the back door. This became our shoe shelf. When the kids take off their school shoes, they now have a place to put them, keeping the back door free from school-shoe debris.

Library books

Our house contains countless books. We have a great stash of our own and we visit the local library regularly to borrow books. While I love having so many books around me, we sometimes found it difficult to track down the school library books. After an hour-long search one evening trying to locate my daughter's missing library book, we developed a better way of looking after the books.

The kids bring school library books home in their library bags, so we decided to place some hooks at the end of the kids' bunk beds. The kids hang their library bags there and when they've read their school library books they place them back in their library bags.

Making schoolchildren independent

To cope with the school environment, kids need to further develop their independence skills. Our kids have shown an increase in self-esteem from being able to successfully complete age-appropriate life skills. I still remember the look of pride on my eldest son's face when he made his first solo train trip into the city. There are other skills he's not so keen to have, such as that of changing his own bed linen. However, as the parent I like to make sure he does whatever he's capable of. Table 7.5 (overleaf) lists some common tasks appropriate for each age group in the primary-school years.

Letting go

Letting go and being prepared for your kids to experience the consequences of their behaviour are important steps in building their independence skills. I often find this concept difficult to apply, and it's something I continue to work on. For example, I now expect all our kinder and school kids to pack their own bags. It's their responsibility to ensure they have their lunchbox, hat and everything else they need for their school day. However, it did take me some time to fully hand over this responsibility to the kids. In my early years as a school mum I could be seen driving forgotten hats to school for the kids.

Keeping track of things

Once you venture into the world of school, you very quickly work out that to stay on top of things you need (1) a way of managing all the incoming dates and (2) a way of tracking all the outgoing items!

Table 7.5: independence skills for school children

Age	Skill
6–8 years old	✳ Wash dishes and/or stack dishwasher
	✳ Know full address
	✳ Tie shoelaces
	✳ Ride a bike
	✳ Tell the key times on an analogue clock
	✳ Buy items at a shop
	✳ Wash own hair
	✳ Pack school bag and organise belongings
	✳ Cook treats such as muffins and slices
8–10 years old	✳ Answer phone and take a message
	✳ Follow multi-step verbal instructions
	✳ Tell the time to the nearest minute on an analogue clock
	✳ Cook a meal
	✳ Change bed linen
	✳ Read a simple map
10–12 years old	✳ Walk home from school on their own
	✳ Stay at home on their own
	✳ Catch public transport
	✳ Make their own school lunchbox

A family calendar

We've been using a family calendar for about five years and I've found it the best way of managing all the kids' activities.

When kids get birthday-party invitations or special-event notices from school, I ask them to write the details under the correct date on the calendar. I've also taught them to adopt the habit of checking the calendar regularly themselves. It's helpful to have little alerts from the kids about upcoming events. If our preschooler has a big event coming up that he's excited about, we even write a countdown for the last few days for him. I love showing him the calendar and asking him to work out 'how many sleeps until ...' by himself!

Visual, visual, visual — see it, appreciate it, acknowledge it, enjoy it, and REMEMBER! A message board at child level encourages my children to take personal responsibility for their own important dates, invitations and school information.

Jane Vanden Boom, mum of three

Children's diaries

A diary is a great self-management tool for kids in middle- to upper-primary school. They can use it to track their reading, homework and sporting commitments.

Label everything!

I think every family has one child who always comes home with less gear than they went to school with. Growing up in my family, believe it or not, I was that child. Being organised is something I've grown into.

We have one of these children in our family and he's been that way ever since he started school. Having all his items clearly labelled doesn't magically bring them home, but it does make it so much easier to find things again. More specifically, it makes it easier for him to find his things again. When we realise something's missing, I try hard to make it his responsibility to locate the item. I've found youngsters tend to hunt distractedly through the lost property bins, so if they have a familiar label on all of their school gear they can find what they're looking for more easily.

Taking action

- If you have a child starting school for the first time, take a low-key but planned approach to their transition.

- Create individual school schedules for each child to help them organise themselves.

- Create a process for staying on top of the constant flow of paperwork from the school.

- Gather the essential details needed to fill in the kids' school forms and compile them into a reference sheet.

- Decide how many after-school activities your children should do.

- Manage your daily routines around the after-school activities so the impact on your younger children is minimised.

- Follow your child's lead and establish a homework routine that suits their personality.

- Put in place infrastructure that will help the kids keep their school gear organised.

- Continue working with your kids to build their independence skills.

- Teach your children to take responsibility for being organised for school and to be prepared for the consequences as they learn to do this.

- Use simple tools to keep track of school dates and the kids' belongings.

Part III

Enjoying parenthood

Chapter 8

You

Being a parent can change how you see and take care of yourself. There's no official start and end time to your day, and there are no holidays or long-service leave. It's a role that you're always in. It took me a few years to work out that I needed to be proactive in determining how I operated as a parent and how I balanced other aspects of my life.

Our family life can be busy. I could spend all my time just getting everyone through the day fed, clothed and cared for. However, spending all my time focusing on the 'now' made me feel as though I was always in catch-up mode when it came to the kids' development. I was reacting to the ever-changing stages of childhood without much forethought, and without a view towards the long-term impacts of the strategies I was using. The turning point for me was reading a book that showed how different things could be if I spent time investigating the type of parent I wanted to be.

I found it tricky adjusting from full-time work to full-time stay-at-home mum. But I found keeping to a routine for me a useful way of managing my time—from set days for changing the sheets to allocated time to exercise and socialise. This ensured that I was not only motivated to keeping things running at home (which can be difficult when you're exhausted), but also that I had time set aside for things that were important just for me.

Catherine Sangster, mum of three
<www.keepcatebusy.blogspot.com>

Defining your guiding principles

Louise Porter has written a fantastic book on young children's behaviour called *Children Are People Too: A Parent's Guide to Young Children's Behaviour* In her book, Porter outlines the guiding principles parents should follow when interacting with their children. They're short, simple statements on how adults can choose to act in the parent–child relationship.

I found the idea of guiding principles powerful and set about creating my own principles of behaviour towards my family. These principles gave me a framework for responding to daily situations in my family life:

• Listen attentively to others.

• Work towards a solution, not someone to blame.

• Show patience—role model the behaviour I want to see.

• Be kind to myself and consider my own needs.

• There is no 'have to' or 'should'—I have a choice.

• It's okay to say 'no'.

• Make time for play.

- Give the children (and adults!) some space and independence.

- There's no need to make comparisons.

- Have a 5:1 ratio of positive to negative comments.

When I use these principles in my interactions with the kids, family life is happier and contains less conflict. Some days I fare better at following them than others. I also find some of the principles more challenging than others. Looking for a solution and not someone to blame requires considerable conscious effort on my behalf. For example, if I enter one of the kids' bedrooms and there has obviously been an altercation that's left debris and a child crying, my first reaction is often to want to know who did this. If I take this path, the kids look to blame each other when explaining themselves to me with excuses such as, 'He pushed me first', or 'He called me names'. None of this is helpful in finding a solution to the problem.

The way young children learn language comprehension they don't pick up the negatives until later. So [when you say] 'don't run inside' what they hear and comprehend is 'run inside', which is confusing for everyone. [It's] much better to say what you want a child to do rather than what you don't want a child to do for so many reasons ...'walk inside' can feel silly when you first [say] it, but once you get used to it, it becomes a habit and is easy.

Kate Fairlie, mum of four <www.picklebums.com>

In these circumstances I have to actively remind myself to focus on helping the children resolve the issue and not dwell on the who, how and why of the incident. Instead of asking 'Who did it?', I should be asking them 'What's the problem?' At first they may give me the same answers as if I asked them who did it, but as I'm not looking for someone to blame, I then guide them into identifying what the actual problem is and what can be done to resolve it.

I have my guiding principles printed out and stuck on the fridge for easy access and regular reflection. On days when I haven't fared so well, I find it useful to read over them once the situation has cooled down and think about how I could have better handled the situation. The guiding principles aren't just confined to my interactions with my family either; they also transfer across to how I operate in general. Establishing the principles makes it easier to deal with new and challenging situations, regardless of who they're with, as I have a reference point I can use for framing my response.

One of the principles in our family is that children and adults are equally courteous to each other and all must remember to say 'please' and 'thank you' (for example, 'Please stop ripping the hall runner').

Liesl Coulthard, mum of two
<www.hoppobumpo.blogspot.com>

A template for guiding principles can be downloaded from <www.planningwithkids.com/resources>.

Setting yearly goals

Now that I had principles that would guide the way I interacted, I needed to start thinking about what I wanted out of my life. Being a parent is a role that I adore, but it's not the only role I have, and there were ideas and dreams that I wanted to invest more time in. I needed to think about what I want to achieve:

- for myself
- with the kids

- with my husband

- for others.

I had so many answers to these questions that I reached a point where I felt almost overwhelmed and disheartened. Here were all these things I wanted to do, but in the mix of raising five kids, how was I going to achieve any of them? I took a step back and realised that many of these were long-term goals, some of which I wouldn't be able to even contemplate until the kids were older. What I needed to do was narrow in on my priorities for the immediate future, and which goals would be achievable over the coming year.

This was the start of a yearly goal-setting process. Using a technique I'd learned in my working life, I took the SMART approach to determining my goals.

Specific. I had to narrow the focus of my goals. They needed to be clear and definitive in their meaning.

Measurable. In the past when setting goals I had made general statements such as 'learn to say no'. Now I had to find a way of measuring that statement. Changing the goal to something specific and measurable, such as 'complete Project A and B before taking on any new commitments' has allowed me to measure how I've progressed.

Attainable. My goals needed to take into account my current workload and known events for the coming year. They had to challenge me out of my comfort zone, but not be set so high that from day one I'd feel I couldn't meet them.

Realistic. I needed to set goals that reflected my ability, time restraints and available funds.

Time bound. Most of the goals would have a one-year time frame; however, some of them may need more specific time frames—for example, 'Save for flights to Sydney by July'.

It took me a couple of years to build better goal statements for myself. Some years my goals resembled vague wish lists rather than a plan for the coming year.

With practice, I'm getting better each year at setting goals. Here's what my 10 goals for this year look like:

- Launch a new blog and relaunch two smaller ones together by the end of March.

- Begin creating video content for the blog by February.

- Go to the Aussie Bloggers Conference in Sydney on 19 March.

- See a band once a quarter with my friends.

- Go out to dinner once a quarter with the family.

- Take the family bushwalking twice during the year.

- Have a weekend away with my husband (no kids!) by May.

- Host one dinner party for eight by the end of the year.

- Donate food to the Asylum Seeker Resource Centre quarterly.

- Visit or call our nanas monthly.

A template for yearly goals can be downloaded from <www.planningwithkids.com/resources>.

Monthly planning and review

The very first time I set myself yearly goals, I was conscious of them for the first month or two. Then, as we waded further into the year, they began slipping off my radar. New opportunities and adventures had come my way and I'd lost my focus on some of the things I'd set myself to achieve. By the end of the year, when I looked at my list there were very few goals I'd succeeded in achieving.

This highlighted to me something I already knew—once set, goals won't achieve themselves. I needed to revisit them regularly, review my progress and—most importantly— take action. So, each month I began revisiting my yearly goals and assessing what I had to do to achieve my goals. Each month I'd list the key tasks I had to complete in order to help me achieve my yearly goals. I'd also add any ad hoc tasks that were a priority for the month. I had created my own monthly review and used it as a method for focusing my energies on my main goals for the year.

I set monthly tasks using the SMART principles as well. After overwhelming myself in the first few months with more than 10 tasks per month, I now limit them to four or five per month. These tasks aren't overly complicated or strategic, but they're clear, tangible and action-oriented. In a busy month such as November (in the lead-up to Christmas), this is what my monthly plan might look like:

- Make an extra set of handmade Christmas gifts.

- In the first week, reorganise my Christmas plans to reduce my workload.

- Send out Christmas cards by the end of the month.

- Get out! Take time to socialise with friends at least twice.

A mum's health and happiness is vital! Plan some time into your week to make yourself happy—whether it's a coffee and chat with good friends or some de-stressing exercise it's always worth the effort.

Belinda Burr, mum of three

Finding time for you

Setting goals and then finding you don't have the time to devote to achieving them is incredibly frustrating. However, over time I've realised that it's possible to achieve them, and that it begins with me and taking care of myself.

A significant part of taking care of myself is making sure I have time to self-reflect, follow my goals and be involved with society, and not only with my family. How I go about accomplishing this will most likely be different from how you or anyone else does, but that doesn't matter—it's not what you do that's important; it's the fact that you're actually investing time in yourself and attaining some balance in your life.

I wrote earlier about the importance of routines in family life. Routines can sound limiting, but they actually allow greater freedom. The only way I've managed to have time for myself and achieve my goals is by including 'time out' in my weekly plan. Before I did that, I struggled to find time for myself. Family life is about compromise: as the primary carer, I can't just do as I please all the time, but I shouldn't have to continually put my own interests behind everyone else's either.

Weekly plan

For three years around the time our fourth son was born, my husband was studying for his Master of Business. This required numerous hours of study time each week, yet he remained cognisant of my needs, which we considered and factored in. This was the first time in my life as a mum that I put together my own weekly plan.

My weekly plan allowed for a couple of trips to the gym during the week and one on the weekend, as well as a sleep-in on

Sunday morning. I printed out the plan and hung it on the fridge where the whole family could see it, and they were committed to helping me achieve my goals.

My husband worked in the city and at peak times could work quite late. We had an agreement that on my gym nights he would be home by 7.30 pm. If he wasn't going to be home on time, he'd give me as much notice as possible, so I could arrange another time for the gym. Having this verbal arrangement made a big difference to my getting to the gym regularly.

This scheduling experience taught me that if I'm serious about having my needs met I have to be proactive. Table 8.1 is an example of a weekly plan that I follow. It shows specifically what I want to achieve and where I need the family's help.

Table 8.1: weekly plan

Activity	Mon.	Tues.	Wed.	Thurs.	Fri.	Sat.	Sun.
Gym		6 am– 7 am		6 am– 7 am			8 am– 9 am
Blog and online activities	8 pm– 10 pm	8 pm– 10 pm	8 pm– 10 pm		8 pm– 10 pm		12 pm– 3 pm 8 pm– 10 pm

The times listed won't be met precisely; however, as these activities become part of my daily routine, they actually do start to happen. I make it to the gym three times a week and have time for blogging. (Note that blogging is now a part-time job for me, which is why it has so many hours allocated to it!) I have to be flexible as circumstances can change. However, having scheduled times has meant that not having time to myself is the exception and not the rule.

You may have no interest in going to the gym or blogging, but you may well have other interests you'd like time to pursue. Try sitting down with your partner and allocating times during the week that will be dedicated to your desired pursuits. Once you've created your weekly plan, take the time to sit with your children and explain it to them—at least to those who are old enough to understand. Your plan may change the children's daily routine so they deserve forewarning. If the kids aren't used to you taking time out for yourself, it's the perfect opportunity to explain what you're doing and why. It's important for kids to understand that you have needs too, and while you're very happy to run them around and support their endeavours, you expect similar support from them with your own.

When/if family come to stay with you pre-book in you time (for example, book a massage, haircut, lunch with a friend, dinner and movie with [your] partner) and tell the family what days they are babysitting.

Kyrstie Barcak, mum of two

A template for a weekly plan can be downloaded from <www.planningwithkids.com/resources>.

Why time for you is so important

As the primary caregiver for our family, I find the mood of our house tends to revolve around my mood. If I'm tired, snappy or lacking in energy, the kids feed off this: there's more bickering among them, there's less cooperation and they can find it difficult to amuse themselves. My mood is directly affected by how much time on my own I can squeeze into the week.

An important activity for keeping my mood positive is staying fit and healthy. For you it could be scrapbooking, crafting or volunteering. Whatever the pursuit, having time to yourself will help improve your mood, which in turn benefits the whole family. Going to the gym has direct benefits for me and indirect benefits for the family:

- *It makes me less cranky.* I can be very grumpy when I leave the house, but after the endorphins kick in on the treadmill, I begin to feel much happier and bring this mood home with me.

- *I sleep better.* The better I sleep, the less tired and cranky I am.

- *I have more energy.* Running around with five kids can get pretty tiring. I find regular exercise gives me stamina to get through the days.

- *I have time for my own thoughts.* I put on my iPod and I don't have to answer any questions or worry about the needs of others for an hour!

Going to the gym isn't the only way I re-energise myself. Socialising and non–child related activities have a similar effect on my mood. I make sure I schedule time for these activities, and although they may only take place once every few months, when combined with exercise they give my life the variety I need to stay healthy, happy and sane.

The burnt chop

Back in my early corporate days I attended a self-improvement workshop specifically designed for women. My memory of the workshop is vague, with the exception of an analogy that the trainer made. She said mothers often gave themselves the 'burnt chop': if they overcooked a chop while cooking dinner, they'd eat the burnt chop themselves. In other words, mothers put everyone else's needs above theirs.

This analogy has stuck with me over the years. There have been (and will probably continue to be) instances where I forgo things that I'd like to do in order to fit in all of my family's needs. Compromise is always necessary within families, but planning time for myself has made these instances far fewer. Taking the burnt chop every time is not the example I want to set for my family. Setting my own goals, and allocating time for myself to achieve them, shows my kids the way I'd like them to behave as they get older.

Taking action

- Define the principles that will guide how you interact with your family.

- Use the SMART approach to set 10 goals for the year.

- Set monthly tasks that will help you progress and achieve your goals for the year.

- Review your progress each month to keep yourself accountable.

- Create a weekly plan that allocates time to your own interests and helps you achieve your goals.

- Discuss your weekly plan with the family and win their support so you actually get the time you've planned for yourself.

- Remember to share around the burnt chop!

Chapter 9

Your partner

My husband works full time in a corporate job in the city. Although his work hours vary, he usually leaves the house at 7.30 am and returns around 7.00 pm. Thankfully, it's only on very rare occasions that he has to work on weekends. His working hours mean we have to make the most of the short time together in the evenings before the kids go to bed. Routines shine here! Having the younger kids bathed and in their pyjamas ready for bed when he comes home means he has time for a cuddle with the toddler before he goes off to bed and time to chat and read stories with the older kids.

My husband has always willingly participated in caring for our kids, but over the years his interactions with them has increased. As the primary carer I've played a significant role in increasing and guiding his involvement. Not every family has two parents living together, but the tips below on communicating and getting your partner involved can still apply.

Getting your partner involved

The concept of 'letting in' your partner to help you with the kids and household chores seems pretty straightforward, right? Who wouldn't want someone to help them? However, for me it wasn't that easy. In many ways my husband and I had a fairly traditional relationship after I resigned from my paid employment. He went to work and I took care of most things in the home. With each child, my workload increased. By the time we had our third child, I felt I had very little time to get all the household chores done.

If I asked my husband to do something such as vacuum the floors, he was happy to help out, but it wasn't something he'd do of his own accord. I found it frustrating having to ask him to do things that I could clearly see needed doing: if I could see it, why couldn't he? So I didn't always ask; I held out to see whether he would just do it. The scenario ran a bit like this:

- I'd wait for him to see that the floors needed to be vacuumed.

- He'd be oblivious to the fact that the floors needed vacuuming.

- I could no longer tolerate the condition of the floors and would vacuum them myself in a huff and give him the silent treatment as I internalised my frustration.

- He'd have no idea why I was so cross.

- Whatever he did next that I didn't like—no matter how trivial—would make me react in a way completely out of proportion to the actual incident.

- He'd have no idea why I reacted as I did, nor that the state of the floors was my trigger.

This scenario—with slight variations—was played out numerous times in our house. I'm not sure why it took me so long to work out that we simply saw things differently. It wasn't that he was choosing not to be helpful (well, not all the time anyway!). Coming home from work in the evening, he didn't see the house the same way I did. I was at home most of the day. This meant looking at things such as dirty floors for long periods of time, so the fact that they needed cleaning was naturally more of an issue for me.

Once I'd worked out that we saw things differently, my next aim was to work out how to manage this so the workload could be shared—even if it wasn't on his radar.

Allowing your partner in doesn't only relate to household chores, but also to hands-on parenting. Being the primary carer means the children are more familiar with me and — particularly when they're young — want me to be the only one who does things for them. This pattern of behaviour became particularly entrenched when my husband was studying as well as working. During those years I became self-reliant in parenting the kids and they became accustomed to Dad being quite busy most of the time. Once he'd finished studying and was available more often, it took the kids and me a considerable time to adjust and allow him to be more involved in parenting. In essence, I had to take a step back and encourage the kids to rely more on their dad.

Discussing expectations

The best way to allow your partner in and to be more involved is to have regular, open discussions about both his and your own expectations.

Before you go back to work make sure you have a conversation about being organised in advance, such as buying the week's groceries on Sunday, who will cook each night and what cleaning chores each [of you] has. This will ensure there are [fewer] fights about one person doing more than the other.

Simone Anderson, mum of one

Household chores

The first time I discussed my expectations of my husband's contribution to the household cleaning with him, I chose a time when we were both calm, sharing a bottle of wine and talking about how things were operating at home. I had a pretty clear vision of what I wanted, but to ensure his involvement was going to be sustainable I needed to reflect on my views and listen to the way he saw things.

We didn't agree on everything. My standards were different from his, but we found a middle ground that we could both live with. When it comes to cleaning, as I noted in chapter 1, there's a certain basic level of cleanliness and tidiness I need to maintain to keep my stress levels in check. The major issues for me are vacuumed floors, clean toilets and basins, and a clear benchtop. Before this discussion, my husband didn't know how important these issues were to me, and while he thinks vacuuming every day isn't sane, he did happily agree to vacuuming once a week. We also agreed on matters related to other household chores including cooking meals and ironing.

Clearly defining the boundaries around the household chores has significantly reduced the number of disagreements we have over the condition of the house and my husband's contribution to it.

Time with the kids

My husband has thankfully never been one to come home from work and expect to be able to sit in peace for a period of time before engaging with the kids. He's greeted excitedly, and usually jumped upon, the minute he enters the house. He gets changed while talking to the kids and then helps with the bedtime routines. Despite this, our kids still often come to me (even on weekends) rather than seeking him out for assistance with their various needs.

As a dad who travels a lot I think it's really important to spend one-on-one time with each child (quantity as well as quality) doing things together that they really enjoy. For my daughter that might mean just the two of us having breakfast at our local café, or browsing in a bookshop with no time limit. I make sure that I'm an active part of my son's cricket team (attending training when I'm in town, scoring, helping the coach and so on).

Andrew Wilson, dad of two

My husband was the one who chose to raise the matter of how to best manage this situation and get the kids to go to him more often when he was available. He was happy to take on a more active role in parenting on the weekends, but I needed to let him do this. We talked about how I could redirect the kids from me to him and with time I'm getting much better at doing this.

There are some key developmental stages when boys need their dads to take the lead role in parenting. I read many parenting books and often talk about the key learning areas for kids with my husband for two reasons: so he understands what's influencing my parenting style, and to share strategies we could use on the kids. After reading *He'll be OK: Growing Gorgeous Boys into Good Men* by Celia Lashlie, I asked my husband to read the book too as our eldest son is heading towards adolescence and some of the information in the book is particularly relevant to dads.

For various reasons, Lashlie advocates that at the age of 11 or 12—when boys approach adolescence—it's time for Mum to get off 'the bridge of adolescence' and for Dad to step up and take the lead for a while. Lashlie isn't saying that mothers don't have a role to play, but that at this critical time in a boy's life he needs his father more. Our parenting style was not heading in that direction, so I was very glad I read this book when my son was 10. It gave me time to prepare for stepping down and for his dad to step up.

Together, my husband and I began working out ways to transition our involvement with our eldest son, and made sure we had clear expectations of who was doing what. The biggest changes were actually about small things. It's now his dad who discusses with him the tidiness of his bedroom, and who helps him with his homework.

Each year my son and I try and get away for a skiing trip (daughter is invited too but not interested). Although skiing is expensive, by staying in budget accommodation we can manage it. Skiing (or some other active outdoor pursuit) is great because we are in a totally different environment from home, developing physical skills and being rewarded with a sense of achievement every day.

Andrew Wilson, dad of two

Teaching your partner the know-how

In the past I've been guilty of laughing with other mothers about some of the deficiencies in our partners' household skills. While it might be amusing to tell the stories, it doesn't actually do much towards encouraging partners to want to do more in the house, nor does it help them do things better next time. I have to remind myself that I know how to do the household chores because I've learned and practised them. If I want my husband to be involved and do things properly, it's only reasonable that I show him the most efficient way of doing them.

This is where having processes really helps. My husband finds it easy to follow a process, especially if it includes notes! Lunchboxes are a great example of this. Before I had a process in place, there was no way my husband would attempt to prepare lunches: 'Too many moving parts,' he would say. However now, if I'm out in the evening, I have a process for him to follow that allows him to take care of the evening preparation for school lunchboxes.

Doing it his way

My processes can make household chores easier for my husband, but I appreciate that they've been built by me to suit my style, and I can't dictate to him how to do things as we work in different ways. For example, in the evenings I like to work through my list of things to do and then sit down to relax whereas my husband prefers to relax first.

If you get offered a list of what to do, take it—all suggestions have some element of usefulness.

Mark Comer, dad of two

On nights when I head to the study to blog and my husband is on tidy-up duty, I make a conscious effort not to comment or direct him when I take a break from blogging. As hard as that is, interfering with his methods isn't helpful and decreases the level of harmony in the house.

Giving your partner space

We're continually working on teaching the kids to go to their dad for help and guidance (and not always to me) not only so that I'm not constantly in demand, but also because it's disempowering for my husband if I step in regularly when he's completely capable of sorting out an issue on his own. This is a work in progress for me and I sometimes find it difficult not to engage in a situation. Luckily, my husband is pretty quick to quietly let me know if I'm overstepping the mark.

I've also observed that I sometimes unintentionally stop him from taking a more active role with the kids, particularly as he's at work during the week and naturally isn't aware of what's going on at home—for example, preparation for excursions, homework assignments and after-school activities all mainly take place while he's away from home. To keep him informed I give him the forms from school to read.

Increasing your partner's confidence

As you can see, my husband's increased connection to the household chores and the kids has been an evolution. It's taken time and a planned approach to make him more involved. If you're trying to get your partner involved, don't expect too much too soon.

▷ Discuss expectations.

▷ Make small changes to your daily routines to incorporate your partner's involvement.

▷ Build on these changes, working on the areas of his strengths first.

▷ Don't give up. If your partner starts well but then tapers off, don't let things slide back to the old way. Discuss expectations again and work together to get back on track.

▷ Let your partner in and give him the space he needs to be able to participate.

Once my husband was more actively engaged in the running of the household, we decided he should take a couple of days off work to stay home as the primary carer. This didn't happen until our fifth child was born, which was quite recently, but it's the best thing we ever did. I had a project I was working on and needed time to complete. I'd head to the study from 8 am to 6 pm (with breaks) and my husband would do all the things I would usually do: the school runs, the lunches, the cleaning, the washing, the playing, the after-school activities and preparing dinner.

For this to work efficiently we had to be prepared. My husband had to:

▷ know the kids' kinder and school timetables

▷ know the baby's and toddler's routines

▷ be left alone to be the primary carer (which meant I had to stay out of the way)

▷ be given help to learn this new role.

The first few times we did this, I helped out quite a lot, but each time he's been home, he's needed less assistance from me. These sessions have increased his self-confidence with the kids—he now knows the kids' routines better, as well as their general needs and how to meet them. It's been fantastic for me as I've been able to take on other opportunities knowing that he's able to take care of the house and kids if I'm out.

Ask your partner to dedicate time to kids on weekends (for example, take them swimming) and spend one-third of the time on housework, one-third cooking [and] one-third having a nice lunch in peace and a hot cup of tea.

Kyrstie Barcak, mum of two

Creating solo time for your partner

My husband does work hard at his paid work and in helping with household chores. Just as I need time to myself to be able to pursue my interests, so does he. His predominant interests are sports-related: watching sport and taking on his own sporting endeavours. He's a man who likes a challenge. During the past four years he's trekked the Kokoda Track, run a marathon and ridden the 3 Peaks Challenge (a 230-kilometre cycling challenge). These challenges all require extensive training, so we've worked on ways of creating time during our busy weeks for him to prepare.

Whether it's playing a round of golf, going for a run or having a few beers with your mates, it's important that dad stills gets to do this. Most dads still work full time and with that comes long hours and other commitments, so being able to have DAD time becomes crucial.

Cameron Whitford, dad of two

- *Use early mornings.* He would often get up at 5 am on weekends so he could go on a four-hour bike ride and then be home in time to get to the kids' football games.

- *Multitask.* Riding to and from work meant he could get some additional kilometres in. On the way home he could take a detour onto some riding paths and still make it home in time to read the kids a story.

- *Have separate adult outings.* As well as doing things together, sometimes we had to do things separately. He'd catch a football game with his mates, while I might go and see a band with friends.

For us to parent well, we need to make sure we're looking after ourselves and doing things we love and that make us happy. By taking time to schedule individual time into our weeks, we've been able to keep some of our own identities, which can so easily be lost among the heavy time demands of a young family.

Taking action

- Discuss expectations with your partner about household chores and interaction with the kids.

- Spend time defining your parenting roles, allowing space for each parent.

- Make time to teach your partner how to do the household chores.

- Build your partner's confidence by giving them time to respond to the kids' needs without your involvement.

- Allocate times on the weekend when your partner is the 'go-to' person for the kids.

- Create time during the week for your partner to pursue their own interests.

Chapter 10

The joys of parenting

Parenting is a team approach in our family. Even with all the plans and processes in the world, if only I follow them, the chances of implementing them successfully are very slim. A coordinated approach to interacting with the kids has meant that while our parenting skills certainly aren't perfect, we've been able to achieve greater family harmony.

A planned approach to parenting

We've taken a planned approach to parenting our kids. This doesn't just mean planning meals, routines and the like. We also take time to think about the way we want to parent: which strategies we'll use and how we'll work together. As kids grow in bursts, so do the behavioural challenges they throw at you. Being prepared for each new developmental stage has really helped us to keep on top of things. I do most of the reading, research and observation of parenting methods, but I don't always have the answers. As the kids grow older and we reach new stages, I'm frequently faced with situations that are completely new to me and I'm unsure how to handle them.

[Planning could include] frequent, preferably weekly, diary meetings to record everyone's commitments and to work out the gaps to enable planned spontaneity. This planning should also include who can cover special events like children who are ill, school sports days, curriculum days and school excursions so that both parents share the benefits and workload of these events.

Julie Holden, mum of two

When faced with these situations, my first reference point is always my husband, just as I am his first reference point. If we can't come up with an approach that works, I seek out more information. Our planned approach to parenting looks something like this:

- We realise we have an ongoing issue that's causing problems at home or need to make a decision on how to handle the developmental behaviour of one of our children.

- We discuss the issue, and if we're unable to come up with a solution, we look further.

- I use parenting books, podcasts and blogs, or ask other parents for ideas for resolving our issue.

- We read and assess the information, and decide how to apply it to our family.

- We discuss the changes we need to make and why. We come to an agreed position and decide whether someone will lead the change.

- We talk to the kids if the changes will affect them. Then we implement the changes.

In the busyness of daily life it sometimes takes longer for us to work out that there's an underlying issue that needs addressing. For example, when our second child was about three and a half, we found some of his behaviour very difficult to deal with. We were parenting him the same way we had our first son, but the strategies we were using to calm him down when he had a tantrum just weren't working. After one particularly exhausting episode, we realised we had to find a different way to work through his tantrums.

That's when I first discovered Louise Porter's book, *Children Are People Too: A Parent's Guide to Young Children's Behaviour*. Her strategy for bringing a child in close when they lose control of themselves resonated with me. It took some discussion to convince my husband to try this technique. However, in order for it to work, we both had to use it every time our son had a tantrum. We also had to explain to our son how we'd be reacting to his behaviour. We let him know that every time he started to carry on we would pick him up and sit, holding him, until he calmed down.

It took many long sessions of sitting with him, and there were many moments when either my husband or I felt like giving up, but by sticking to this new approach we eventually had success. We'd found a way to help our child safely through his tantrum and minimise the impact it had on everyone else in the house.

Making time for your relationship

The healthy relationship that my husband and I share exists because it receives nourishment and attention. Family life with young children can be exhausting at times. It takes considerable energy to feed, love and care for youngsters. However, for our family to be cohesive and happy, we have to make sure that as a couple we're putting time and energy into our relationship.

Sometimes it can feel like there isn't much energy left at the end of the day for anything other than getting ready for bed!

On those days it takes a conscious effort on my part to take an interest in my husband's day and to step away from my inward focus. Despite this, I feel so much better afterwards, and it keeps our relationship thriving.

Like cars need a service, so do relationships sometimes. If things are not so good, like cars, take it to get a service. There is no shame in getting some help, whether it is from a counsellor, friend or even a good book for tips.

Kerry Knight, mum of four

Communicating with your partner

Communicating with your partner sounds quite obvious, doesn't it? During the week I have a very clear idea of what I'm doing and I just assume my husband does as well. In reality, his focus is different from mine, and he may not be at all aware of what's going on in my part of the world. Not keeping each other up to date on what we're doing can easily lead to confusion. For example, one evening I went to a girlfriend's house with the kids for an early dinner not knowing that my husband had left his keys at home. He assumed I'd be home and I assumed he was working late (as he had been all week). His unexpected early finish at work saw him waiting in the cold outside the locked house!

We also find it incredibly useful to take time for talking about what's on our to-do lists. From these discussions we determine whether we have any crossovers and how we can help each other out. To help us communicate effectively we:

- chat each night once the kids are in bed about major upcoming commitments and activities

- use email to send each other information about dates and significant events

- use the family calendar to mark out nights that we'll be out on our own.

I've learned that my husband may not always be aware of how I'm feeling. He's become much quicker at noticing that something's wrong, but it's difficult for him to work out whether I'm okay among the organised chaos of the evening rush. I can wait for him to ask me how I'm going (or get slightly frustrated with him if he doesn't), or I can just tell him how I'm feeling. If how I'm feeling is directly related to him, he can discuss this with me. If it's unrelated, he can offer support and advice. Either way, communicating with him can help eliminate potential conflict.

Naturally, the same applies to my husband: he lets me know if anything is bothering him and what we can do to remedy this.

We touch base on a weekly basis on how we're currently feeling — work, where our mental space is and our family life. We then talk about what would help our partner deal with the week ahead (for example, take the kids out for a few hours to give our partner some downtime).

Laine Yates, mum of two
<www.blog.icklekids.com.au>

Planning time alone together

The concept of planned, regular 'date nights' is hugely popular at the moment, and while I love the idea, it hasn't always been practical for us to implement. With a new baby and a number of young children, the idea of regularly organising a babysitter so we can go out — in addition to other social commitments with friends, school and kinder — actually seemed like hard work to me. For a few years when we were living in the inner city we had a subscription to the theatre.

This meant every six to eight weeks we went to see a play. However, during the last year that we had the subscription I ended up seeing a play on my own as it had become difficult to line everything up.

We're fortunate to have some family in Melbourne who generously help us with babysitting. However, it's generosity that I don't wish to overuse. An alternative to going out for us is to have a night in—a night where we let go of the household chores, put on some music, grab a drink and enjoy each other's company. With the kids settled in bed, it's refreshing to spend this time alone having an adult conversation. I particularly love it in summer when we can sit outside on the warmer evenings.

Regardless of how you do it, it's important to find time in the family schedule for parents to relax together. As our youngest child gets older, I can see how it will be easier to organise a regular night out on our own, but we aren't quite there yet.

Every year we try to get away as a couple. This year we went to Sydney for two nights with just the baby. It is the most divine thing in the world to spend time alone, and remember what first attracted you to your partner and what you have that is special together. It is time well spent that has a wonderful flow-on effect to the rest of the family. The children always miss us (and us them!), but they have a wonderful time and have many stories to share with us on our return.

Katie McIntosh, mum of eight

Preparing for the evening peak hour

It helps for parents to work as a team, especially at times when not doing so can have a big impact on family harmony. One of these times is the peak-hour evening rush. I heard an ABC podcast called 'managing stress' that said research shows that the first hour after the second parent arrives home in the evening is a high-risk time for disagreement and conflict between parents. This can increase the stress levels of the family by flowing on to the kids

Inspired by the research, over the past year I've made a conscious effort to set aside any negative comments or complaints for the first hour after my husband comes home. This restraint has made a big difference to how the rest of the evening flows.

In the past, in the heat of rush hour, I've been known to vent the first moment my husband walks through the door. An example is if I'd asked him to fix a kitchen cupboard, and he hadn't yet had a chance to do it. Before he came home, I'd spend considerable time trying to get the equipment I needed for preparing dinner out of the cupboard. Meanwhile, the older children would start to fight and the toddler would cry incessantly because he was tired and wanted to be held. All these factors converge, and I see the cupboard as the main cause of the situation, which—of course—it isn't.

In a scenario such as this one, when my husband walks in the door, I'm still frustrated over the situation so I blurt out to him within the first few minutes that I 'wasted 15 minutes on the cupboard and doing so caused all sorts of other annoying things to happen'. He feels attacked and is on guard from the moment he arrives home. The kids pick up on this bad vibe and may choose to talk about the negative aspects of their day rather than focusing on the fun things that happened. The evening peak-hour rush is descending further into negativity.

Nowadays our evening routine looks more like this:

- My husband arrives home.
- He has a general chit-chat with the kids.
- We get the kids off to bed.

- We have an adult-only discussion about the big and the small issues.

By changing my approach and choosing not to talk about an issue until later in the evening, we're experiencing far less conflict during our evening routine. This doesn't mean I don't communicate my frustration or unhappiness to my husband, but it means I'm choosing the best time and a calmer approach. In reality, in our house it's often much longer than an hour before I get a chance to talk about whatever is bothering me. By then my frustration has dissipated and I can talk about it more calmly. Quite often I don't even bother bringing it up. With the heat out of the situation, I realise it really wasn't such a big deal after all.

This approach requires commitment from my husband too. If he arrives home to a house that looks like a cyclone has blazed a path through it, he realises it's not wise to comment —even in jest—as there's a fair chance I won't see the humour, and this could start the evening off on a negative note.

Preparing for the morning peak hour

Another time when working as a team has a significant impact is during the morning rush hour. Mornings run smoothest for us when there's been adequate preparation the night before. Reducing the workload in the morning decreases my potential stress levels and means I'm better prepared to cope with the unexpected things that so frequently occur with our youngest kids. Preparing the night before without interruption—when the kids are in bed—saves us time as everything only takes half as long to do.

I can't say we always feel like doing these things at night when the kids are in bed, or that we wouldn't prefer to flop down on the couch with a book or watch some TV. However, from past chaotic morning experiences, that 30 minutes of preparation the night before makes all the difference to us having a good start to the day. It also means I can get to the gym some mornings and my husband can ride to work occasionally. Here's what we do in the evening:

- set the table for breakfast

- prepare the lunchboxes

- complete the notices that need to be returned to school

- ensure uniforms and clothes are clean and ready to be worn

- empty the dishwasher

- generally tidy up

- empty the bin/s

- check the family calendar

- write a 'to do' list

- wind down.

Taking action

- Plan how you'll work together with your partner to develop parenting strategies.

- Define key behaviour boundaries for your kids that you both agree on.

- Communicate regularly with your partner about what you're doing and how you're feeling.

- Plan time with your partner when you aren't doing household chores and can enjoy each other's company.

- To keep the peak-hour evening rush conflict-free, plan to talk about any issues when the kids are in bed.

- Create a night-time routine that prepares for the next day.

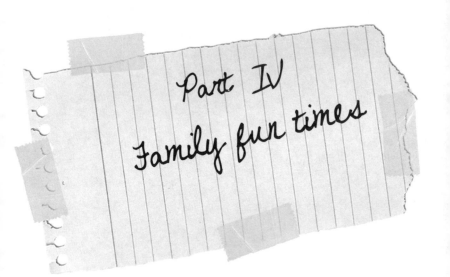

Part IV
Family fun times

Making time for play

The main way for children to investigate their environment and make sense of the world is through play. When you watch children closely as they play, you can see they're doing so much more than just having fun. I'm a strong advocate of the importance of play in a child's life. I think it's very easy to become too serious about life and have high expectations of children. Childhood to me seems to be getting shorter. The coining of the 'tweens' stage of childhood seems to be an example of how children are growing up much more quickly than in previous generations. Children are now given homework early in primary school and the volume of work consumes time they would have once spent playing.

In our family, play is integral for a happy existence. It's soon evident if Mum and Dad have been caught up in too many domestic duties and have neglected actively playing with the kids: the whining increases, there's more bickering and the overall atmosphere of the house is more negative.

When planning our family activities, I aim to include three types of 'fun' time:

- unstructured time at home when the kids occupy themselves

- time at home playing with the kids

- time away from home having fun together.

It often works best to have more kids over. A friend for each of them usually works out less work (and stress) for you. If one sibling is left out, there will inevitably be fighting and tears before bedtime … so take a deep breath and round up a couple more kiddos to tear apart your house!

Catherine Sangster, mum of three
<www.keepcatebusy.blogspot.com>

Giving kids time alone

In recent years I've realised how easy it is to get caught up in after-school activities, weekend sport commitments, play dates and the various other obligations that come with having young children. All of this can result in overstimulated, exhausted children.

It can also result in children expecting to be entertained and occupied all the time. When our eldest son first started kinder, I saw this as the perfect opportunity to spend individual time with our toddler. For the first few weeks, I devoted most of our time alone to playing with him. I soon realised this wasn't practical or in his best interests and decided to lessen the time I spent with him.

At first he really struggled to occupy himself even when I'd set up activities for him. He'd become whiney and wanted to be picked up frequently. It took me a couple of weeks to establish a better play routine. I found he was fresher immediately after kinder drop-off, so I'd encourage him to play by himself at that time. While I took care of the household chores, I'd talk to him and let him help me if he wanted to. Gradually he was able to play on his own for longer periods of time, and I discovered I could sit and play with him for 15 minutes, set up a new activity and he'd play again on his own for a while.

The bonuses of boredom

Older kids can also become dependent on being entertained all the time. I believe children need time to rest, potter and investigate things in their own environment without time pressures. I also think it's great for them to be 'bored' occasionally. Often, this is the only time when our kids seek out new interests, design games of their own and maybe even participate in the household chores without being asked to!

Allowing children to have time when they 'don't have anything to do' can lead to positive results. It's at these times that I see our kids become really creative with their play. They may build amazing constructions out of LEGO or from recycled materials. Sometimes they use this time to find a good book and read. Most importantly they learn to operate at a slow pace. I'm all for productivity and efficiency, but it needs to be coupled with rest and relaxation, and as the parent I like to make sure I'm taking the lead in slowing things down.

Get outdoors whenever possible and join in when you can — you're not always going to be able to keep up with your kids so do it while you can. Encourage your kids to be able to play alone as well as together; [it] stops the 'there's nothing to do' complaints on wet days.

Stephen Fulton, dad of three

Scheduling play

Along with the joys of a large family come additional complexities such as finding time to play despite the increased workload, spending time with each child individually and finding activities that will interests all the kids.

Building play into the everyday

One of the beautiful things about play is that it can be done almost anytime, anywhere, and with no resources or with an amazing array of objects. In the busy bustle of our days, without some conscious effort it can be easy for play to be overlooked. This is not only to the kids' detriment, but to mine too. It's surprising how invigorated and happy I feel when I take even a short time out to play with my kids.

It's possible to include play in our daily routines without too much difficulty, which makes a huge difference to my relationship with the kids, and my mood. The list below includes some examples of how I've turned repetitive aspects of daily life into playful fun:

- *Morning tea.* Take a blanket outside and have a picnic. If it's a rainy day, make it an inside picnic. Enlist the children's help to gather the supplies.

- *Cleaning.* Vacuuming the house can be a lot of fun if your children aren't frightened of the vacuum cleaner. As the vacuum cleaner is making its way around the house, it can go out of control and suck up little children! My children often try to dodge the head as I push it around the carpet. It may take me a bit longer to get the vacuuming done, but it's fun.

- *Laundry.* While sorting the laundry (mine does pile up at times), you can hide a child underneath a pile and pretend you can't find them. While hanging towels and sheets on the line, you can also play peek-a-boo.

- *Lunch.* Play 'Restaurants'. Create a menu. Select a chef and waiting staff; then set the table and enjoy lunch at your home restaurant.

- *Tidy up.* Allow toys to take on personalities and help them find their homes. For example, 'Thomas the Tank Engine is sad. He needs to find Annie and Clarabel — let's find his friends so he can go to sleep'. Or 'Teddy is confused. He thinks his place is in the bathroom, but does he belong there?'

- *Bath.* The bath can be a great place for play: pouring water, blowing bubbles and splashing, for example. We have a range of pouring toys such as jugs and tea sets in the bath and the kids often make me cups of tea.

Making the effort to take a playful approach to household chores lightens both the kids' and my mood. When the kids are in a better mood, there's more cooperation and less fighting.

Individual time with each child

Making sure I spend enough time alone with each child with the sole focus of playing is my biggest challenge. As a mum of five kids I do expect my kids to entertain themselves, but I also be-lieve they need regular time where my attention is fully focused on them individually. The more children I have had, the trickier this has become, but there are some ways to make it a bit easier.

Every week one child is allotted two hours on a weekend to spend with either parent. Outings have been the movies, bike riding, park, football or cricket. The child loves the one-on-one time and particularly the planning of their outing.

Katie McIntosh, mum of eight

I don't implement all of the strategies every day; however, during most weeks I'm able to achieve individual time with each of the kids. There are those weeks when the toddler is sick, or I have a number of commitments and don't spend as much time as I'd like one-on-one with them. It's not possible to 'catch up' on this time, and I've learned not to stress over this. I just take the next week as a clean slate and try again to spend individual time with each child.

Scheduled bed times

Our children's ages currently range from two to 12 years, so—as I mentioned earlier—we have different bed times according to age. As each child goes to bed, it's easier to spend time individually with the remaining kids—it can be something as simple as reading their bedtime story with them or having a chat.

One-on-one play time

I schedule one-on-one play time with my kids and I find it's a wonderful thing to do. The way it works is that I allocate 20 minutes to each child, during which time they can choose what they want to do and what they'd like me to do. This time is completely child-led. The kids can also choose to let the other kids play with us. Sometimes the activity they choose may naturally preclude the others from playing as it's a two-person game, such as chess. However, if it's an open activity such as dress-ups they may be happy for their siblings to join in, but they still lead the direction of play.

The best gift you can give your child is time—your time—to be completely present in the moment with them to care, nurture, encourage, play, laugh and above all love.

Caroline Comer, mum of two

I actually set the timer on my phone and the kids know that once the timer goes off, that's the end of the session. This really helps with the younger ones, who would love me to continue playing all day. Sometimes they still take it hard when their play time comes to an end, but it's important for them to understand that each child deserves a turn.

School holidays are the perfect time to schedule play time. Weekends can be too, depending on what we have on. The kids' behaviour is often a cue for me that I need to do more playing. Constant complaining, grumpiness and other testing behaviours generally indicate that the kids need some time with their dad or me on their own.

Unplanned opportunities

There are times when our toddler is asleep and the older kids are playing happily or doing something together. I take this opportunity to spend time chatting or playing with our preschooler on his own.

Or, in the case of our early-rising toddler, some mornings I take advantage of everyone else being asleep and use that opportunity to play with him.

Play time for different ages

With the age gap between our eldest and youngest children being so great, organising fun time for all our kids takes a bit of organisation. Choosing activities for school holidays, outings on weekends and what we watch on TV are just some of the challenges we face when deciding how to entertain all the age groups at the same time. Some strategies we use for managing this are:

- letting the older children stay home
- splitting the family up

- having separate activities in the same place
- organising family activities.

Letting the older children stay home

There are times when I'm happy to leave our older boys (nine and 12 years old) at home on their own. If we have a short, local gathering (such as a preschool reading session or a craft lesson) to attend nearby that's not suitable for the older children, I'll let them stay home and only take the younger ones.

Splitting the family up

There are times when the family splits up to attend events and activities. For example, my husband may take the older boys to a night game of football. As it starts at 7.30 pm and is in winter, it doesn't suit the younger kids. I'll stay home with the younger ones and we do something together, such as hire a DVD and eat popcorn.

Separate activities — same place

This is a more recent strategy for me, and it's heavily dependent on where we are. This works when we're at events with activities that are suitable for a range of age groups. Instead of dragging everyone to each activity and having either the younger or older kids wait the activity out, I let the older kids go off by themselves. I take the younger kids to their activity and then we meet up at an arranged time and place.

For example, I once took all five kids to the Moomba festival on my own. The activities that suited the younger kids were not at all appealing to the older boys. To ensure everyone had fun, I stayed with the three youngest while they had turns on the clowns. The two eldest boys went to line up for a roller-coaster ride. Once we'd finished at the clowns we waited by the roller coaster for it to finish.

Parents have differing comfort levels when it comes to allowing their kids to do things on their own. It's always important to take into account the personalities of the kids and the environment they will be in.

Family activities

There are also outings to places of interest to all ages that can be enjoyed together as a family. These include:

- zoos and animal sanctuaries
- art galleries
- parks
- bushwalks
- the beach or pool.

There are also activities you can do at home that can be tailored to suit all skills and abilities, such as:

- LEGO
- construction with a glue gun and/or nails and screws
- hide-and-seek
- bike riding
- footpath chalk drawing
- football and cricket.

Expecting understanding

There are also times when you have to attend events that don't suit everyone. I talk regularly to all the kids about the need for understanding in our family and that we have to balance competing needs. It's important to remind the older boys that their younger siblings have been tagging along to their activities since they were born. I also remind them that when they were younger they didn't have to do this, and that the younger children deserve the same opportunities. When we do attend an event for the younger kids, I allow the older kids to bring a book to read, if appropriate, so that they're occupied. I also remind them that it's important for them to allow the little ones to enjoy themselves without having to put up with their complaining.

Organising the kids' toys

For kids, a big part of play is their toys, and it's amazing how quickly toys accumulate! Finding enough suitable places for storing different kinds of toys where they're out of everyone's way and easy for the kids to access can be quite an ask in families with several kids.

I have three crates. There's always one in the lounge, one in the family room and one stored in a cupboard in the computer room. I switch them [around] every couple of months. I think he would be quite happy with just the one box—it seems junk mail and Tupperware are far more exciting [than] all the expensive toys our family have bought him!

Fern Treacy, mum of three

Storing toys

While I can't ever say that I have the kids' toys fully under control, I have worked out some strategies that help me manage them better.

Toy shelf

Due to the floor plan of our house, we don't have a playroom as such. Toys are kept in cupboards in the children's bedrooms and we have a toy shelf in the family room. The older kids can easily access the cupboards to choose the games or toys they want and then (hopefully) return them. Selected toys belonging to the two youngest children are stored on the toy shelf.

The toy shelf is a successful storage solution for the younger kids' toys because:

▷ *there's a finite number of toys on the shelf.* Too much choice is often difficult for younger children to manage. They're more likely to want to have a go at everything and this just adds up to additional mess, without any real value for the kids. Limiting the number of toys available makes selection easier and reduces mess.

▷ *the kids can choose their toys by themselves.* When I sit down with them to play, or if they're playing by themselves, they can easily make a decision on what they want, find it and take it off the shelf.

▷ *there's a place for everything.* Although I don't expect each toy to go back to the exact spot where I put it, the shelf makes it easy for the little kids to remember where they took the toy from and where they should put it back.

Storing toys (*cont'd*)

▷ *it makes rotating toys easy.* I can draw from the stocks in the cupboards and rotate the toys. The kids get excited about having new toys, and the toys help keep their choices fresh and appropriate for the developmental stage they're at.

Miscellaneous pieces bag

It seems that the older the kids get, the smaller the pieces are for their toys. Once they're over the age where they could chew and swallow small pieces, the kids have toys that have many small parts. Even when they pack up their toys, I always find stray bits and pieces of toys and games. I used to spend lots of time finding the right game and returning the pieces to their respective homes. (I have a slight obsession with making sure the toys and games all have their correct pieces.) It then occurred to me that the kids never worked out they hadn't packed up properly because the next time they grabbed a game to play with all the pieces were there.

At a family meeting I explained to the kids that from that point on when I found stray parts belonging to games and toys, I'd be placing them in the drawstring bag that I'd hung on the wardrobe door handle and that they'd be responsible for putting them back in their rightful place. The kids seemed happy enough with this, mainly as it didn't mean any immediate work for them.

However, they quickly worked out that this system provided a shortcut in their tidying-up process! Within a few weeks the bag was bursting full of all sorts of things. Not to be deterred, I then informed them that each time the bag was full they'd have to empty it. Everything from the bag had to find a home or get thrown out. It took the kids more than an hour to empty the full bag the first time. That experience has significantly reduced how much stuff the kids put into the bag.

Pre-Christmas cull

Each year around October the kids and I undertake a massive reorganisation of all the toys. We go through the toy cupboard, pull everything out and determine what:

▷ needs to be fixed

▷ should be kept

▷ could be thrown away

▷ can be given to charity.

This process gets us prepared for the new toys and games that inevitably arrive over the following months for birthdays and Christmas.

Taking action

• Look at the family schedule and make sure it includes plenty of unstructured time at home for the kids.

• Find time in your daily routine for building in play opportunities with the kids.

• Kids love one-on-one time with parents. Set up weekly routines so there's space for this.

• As children get older, spend some time planning family activities to cater for any differing ages.

• Take a proactive approach to the kids' toys, regularly rotating, organising and culling them.

Chapter 12

Preparing for holidays

Before you leave

Getting everything organised for a family holiday can be time-consuming. It can be tricky to remember everything we have to do before we go, especially at busy times of the year such as Christmas. To avoid having to remember every job from one holiday to the next I created a 'to do' checklist like in table 12.1, which I stick onto the fridge the week before we go away.

Table 12.1: to do before we go on holidays checklist

Job	
Cancel newspaper	☐
Cancel milk deliveries	☐
Arrange garbage collection	☐
Arrange mail collection	☐
Arrange dogsitting	☐

Job	
Clear out the fridge	☐
Empty compost bucket	☐
Empty kitchen bin	☐
Prepare meal plan and shopping list for returning week	☐
Work through washing	☐
Vacuum the house	☐
Turn off appliances at the switch	☐
Check all windows and doors are locked	☐

Make sure you have a day's leave either side of the actual holiday—one for preparation to get you on your holiday and one for recovery at the end before you go back to work.

Sam Dumsday, mum of two

Driving with kids

For us, it makes sense to go on a family holiday by car due to travel costs and the volume of luggage we have to take with us. I have family in Mildura (550 kilometres north-west of Melbourne) so we've driven the Calder Highway to Mildura countless times. Each time, we find some way of refining or improving our preparation for the trip. With breaks along the way to let the children run around, this trip can take us anywhere from six to eight hours. This is a long time for kids to be in a car, so preparation is the key to ensuring that the trip is a fun experience for everyone.

> *We bought a campervan to help us to be able to afford more breaks and holidays. The kids love it and they help organise trips, set up and pack up. Even if it is just an hour down the road, we get to spend time with the kids for the whole weekend, relaxing, playing and talking with the kids.*
>
> Kerry Knight, mum of four

Preparing for a car trip

Before I pack for a long car trip, I write a master checklist of what to take:

- children's clothing
- food packs
- bedding
- important extras
- miscellaneous
- activity packs.

This list is broken into a number of smaller checklists. A downloadable template for each checklist mentioned can be found at <www.planningwithkids.com/resources>.

Children's clothing

We involve the kids in the packing process and ask them to help choose the clothes they should take. Once they've decided, I draw up a checklist for them to use when packing (see table 12.2). As not all the kids can read yet, the checklist has both words and pictures.

When we go on short trips, I ensure we take enough clothes so I don't have to do laundry while we're away. However, when we stay with family I do try to wash so I don't have to take too many dirty clothes home with us.

Table 12.2: children's checklist

Items for a four-day stay	
Underwear × 5	Thongs
Socks × 5	Runners
Pyjamas	Hat
T-shirts × 4	Bathers and goggles
Long-sleeved T-shirt	Beach towel
Jacket or hoodie	Toothbrush
Shorts × 4	Books
Jeans	

Food packs

If we're travelling for more than one and a half hours, we definitely have to take food for the kids. They've made it clear to us that they may starve unless they're fed bi-hourly! We have a people mover, so for logistical reasons—and also to encourage independence in the kids—we make individual food packs. Each child has a backpack in which to store all their items for the trip. We make it clear that the food has to last the entire journey, so they need to pace themselves.

Since we started this a number of years ago, long car trips have been much more peaceful. There are no complaints of 'I'm hungry', 'What's to eat?' or 'I need a drink'. Each child can access their pack and eat whatever they like, when they like. The exception, of course, is our toddler. He hates being left out so we pack him his own backpack as well and the non-driving parent passes his food and drinks to him as he demands them!

As I suffer from motion sickness, it also helps me, as I'm not constantly turning around passing food to the kids, which can often kick off my nausea. If the kids eat junk food while travelling, their behaviour worsens, so I try to keep the food as healthy as possible. I also try to include foods that are low on mess, are filling and are easy for the younger children to manage independently.

The additional positives to packing our own food are that it's cheaper than buying food along the way and it gives us greater flexibility with regard to stopping for breaks during the trip. If they're sleeping, our little ones tend to wake up if the car stops so we're happy not to have to stop. This way our breaks are not dependent on finding a place to buy food—only somewhere with toilet facilities and space for the kids to stretch their legs. Table 12.3 lists a typical food pack.

Table 12.3: food pack for six-hour road trip

Food item	Notes
Salad rolls	Two for the older kids; one for the younger kids
Crackers	Plain crackers such as water crackers, rice cakes and Cruskits
Cereal	Dry cereal can be a great snack, for example, Mini Weats, or Weet-Bix Crunch
Fruit	Apples, bananas, mandarins and grapes are all easy fruits to eat in the car
Mixed nuts	We have no nut allergies in the family, and nuts are an easy snack to pack
Homemade popcorn	Air-popped with no additives
Veggie sticks	Capsicum, carrot, celery, cucumber, beans and snow peas are all easy, mess-free veggie sticks the kids can munch on in the car
Homemade treats	I find chocolate balls, lemon slice, 100s of biscuits and Rice Bubble slice are the least messy homemade snacks for the car
Water bottle	I make sure that if they have lids the younger children can manage on their own
Rubbish bag	A plastic bag with ties they can place all their scraps and wrappers in
Wet face cloth	I wet a face cloth and place it into a small plastic bag. The kids can then keep themselves clean as they need to
Tissues	Someone is sure to need them!

The kids aren't the only ones who need refreshments on a long drive. As far as food goes, my husband and I prepare very similar packs for ourselves as we do for the kids (only much less). We take water, but I like to pack some cold drinks as well. We make our own ice packs by placing ice-cream containers of water in the freezer for a few days beforehand to use during the trip for keeping the drinks cold. Whenever we've travelled with a baby we also used these ice packs to keep their food fresh.

Bedding

When we travel we often stay with family. As there are a few of us, we usually have to bring along sleeping paraphernalia such as pillows, sleeping bags, camping stretcher and a port-a-cot. A couple of the kids also have comforters (blankets) of some description, so it's important for my sanity that they're packed too.

Important extras

If we're going away for a particular celebration such as Christmas or Easter, I prepare a list of everything we need to take for the occasion (Christmas presents, Easter eggs and so on). If we're going camping I list all the gear we'll need, such as a tent, camping stretchers, torches, cooking implements and an esky.

Miscellaneous

Although we could survive without the items listed in table 12.4, they do ensure that our time away is as stress-free and fun as possible.

Table 12.4: Miscellaneous items

Item	Notes
Camera	Battery charger
Mobile phones	Chargers
Basic medicines	Children's Panadol, bandaids, Savlon
Everyday bag	Goes everywhere with me
Sunscreen and insect repellent	Small roll-ons are perfect for using in the car
Street map	Even if you know the way, it's handy to have in the car in case of detours for flooding, etc.
Sunglasses	Driving into glare is never fun
Motion-sickness pack	I like to make sure we have a towel and plastic bag within easy reach just in case
Emergency stash	Although I prefer our kids to eat healthily, I also like to have a secret emergency stash of non-melting treats in the car, just in case we hit desperate times!
Audio books and CDs	Audio books and CDs can be very calming in the car because the children are quiet as they listen

The most two used items and the ones I always had in my handbag or pocket when travelling were a small tube of Papaw ointment and some bandaids! Great for stopping potential tears, giving a tired kid a bit of TLC, for chapped lips, and even lubricating an arm that was stuck in the cup holder at the movies!

Natasha Key, mum of three

Activity packs

Individual activity packs (see table 12.5, overleaf), help children to pass the time on long journeys. Our kids can access them whenever they want to. They each choose what goes into their pack so we're quite sure they contain plenty of things that will entertain them.

Table 12.5: children's activity packs

Item	Notes
Books	We pack a couple of their favourites. Even if they can't read in the car (I can't as I suffer from motion sickness), they can be read as their bedtime stories while we're away.
Travel game	This is for the older children. Mini versions of the bigger games, or hand-held puzzles (ones which don't have small parts that will get lost in the car) are perfect for this.
Favourite toy	This is for the younger children—something small without lots of small parts.
Homemade workbook	I get the children to help me put these together to make sure they're age-appropriate and have activities they will enjoy.
	They contain some or all of the following:
	✳ spot-the-sign game
	✳ a map with our journey marked out
	✳ mazes
	✳ colouring-in pages
	✳ spot the difference
	✳ addition and subtraction worksheets
	✳ dot-to-dots
	✳ word searches
	✳ brain teasers
	✳ quizzes.
	For templates and website links on how to make your own activity books, see <www.planningwithkids.com/resources>.

Surviving the car trip

Once we've organised everything at home, made our checklists and ticked everything off, it's finally time to head off. With five kids confined to the space of a car for upwards of six hours, we need to have a few strategies up our sleeves to ensure the family car trip doesn't turn into a nightmare.

Car ventilation

Even when travelling in cold weather, I've found that to keep everyone feeling as fresh as possible, you need to have adequate ventilation and fresh air coming into the car throughout the trip. We found that out the hard way!

We've had a people mover for several years, having bought the new vehicle a couple of days before we headed to Mildura for Christmas one year. We went through our usual packing process and were on the road by mid morning. It was a very warm summer's day and we'd only travelled for a bit more than 30 minutes when our eldest child, who was sitting in the back, threw up (not the ideal start to a family holiday). After cleaning him up and then cleaning the car, we asked him how he was feeling and whether he had any idea why he was sick. 'I was hot and stuffy', was his response. It turned out there was a separate switch for turning on the air vents in the back of the car that we didn't know about. We hadn't turned them on and it was very stuffy for the kids at the back, which caused him to feel nauseous. This is now one of the first things I check when we embark on a long journey!

Sun protection

We don't have tinted windows or fancy shades for the car to block out the sun. As with ventilation, it can make the journey quite unpleasant for the children if they have the sun beating in

Surviving the car trip (*cont'd*)

on them. We use the old method of placing a light sheet across the window to block out any direct sunlight on the kids.

It's possible to get sunburnt inside cars, and we're particularly mindful of this because our kids are all fair-skinned. Having the kids apply sunscreen in hot weather is essential.

Setting expectations

We tell the kids how long the drive will be and how often we're likely to stop to pre-empt the many questions we would otherwise hear throughout the trip. This also helps them pace themselves regarding what they eat and when. For the older children I print out a map of the route so they can see where we are and which towns are coming up. This gives them a reference point for their location, and helps build their map-reading skills.

Audio books

We have a rotation system in the car for long trips whereby everyone has a turn at choosing a CD. We all love music, but usually, a couple of hours into the trip, someone will request an audio book. When we play one of the older boys' favourite audio books there can be two benefits: they're entertained, and the hypnotic sound of the reader's voice tends to send the little ones off to sleep!

You can find a list of excellent audio books for long car trips at <www.planningwithkids.com/resources>.

Adequate breaks

It can be tempting to drive without stopping to reach the end destination as quickly as possible. However, we've learned that a long trip is more pleasant and memorable if we stop and have rest breaks for the driver and give the kids run-around time.

As we take our own food, we tend to take our breaks at parks, which are more interesting and fun for kids than a roadhouse. We take along a football for the kids to kick, and they use the play equipment and toilet facilities. After a break such as this we all get back into the car feeling invigorated and refreshed.

Interaction

Listening to audio books and working on their activity packs are great ways for kids to pass the time, but the family car trip is a group experience so interaction is a must too. It can be simple things such as discussing landmarks that we pass, or counting the animals we see. Or we play car games such as:

⇨ *car cricket.* You can make up your own rules, but ours go something like this: a red car = 1 run; a truck = 4 runs; a motorbike = 6 runs. The batsman is out if we see an emergency vehicle, are passed by another car or cross train tracks.

⇨ *'I Spy'.* This is popular because it's easy even for our young children to join in.

⇨ *'20 Questions'.* This is a traditional game where one player thinks of something and keeps it to themselves.

Everyone else in the car takes turns asking a question that can be answered with either 'yes' or 'no'. If someone guesses the correct answer, it's their turn to think of something. If 20 questions have been asked and no-one has been able to guess correctly, the answer is revealed and that player has another turn.

When it's just me driving on a long trip, it's so much easier having all the kids' favourite songs on a single playlist on the iPod. The longer the list, the less often the same songs come round again and again.

Cath Taylor, mum of three <www.mobblegobble.com>

Flying with kids

Since growing our family to five children, we've only had a couple of holidays where we've flown to our destination. Each time, to make it easy on the finances, we flew with budget airlines. Taking the cheaper option is doable, but it requires extra planning, especially with kids. I'd like to share with you some tips I learned that make our flights easier and more enjoyable.

If you're going on a long trip, try to have one parent 'on duty' and the other 'on a break'. If you're flying, have the parent on the break sitting in the aisle seat or in a corner resting at a stopover while the other parent on duty takes the children on an adventure around the airport.

Laine Yates, mum of two <www.blog.icklekids.com.au>

Be prepared for delays

Each flight we've taken has been delayed—one in excess of one and a half hours. The budget airlines seem to have only a small margin for error as they turn around flights so quickly. It appears that the domino effect for even small delays can become quite significant and is a routine part of flying with these airlines. For parents this means having extra food supplies and changes of clothes for babies and toddlers. Once, while waiting for a flight to Sydney, my toddler poured water over one set of clothes. Then, to my horror, while waiting in the very crowded departure lounge he had diarrhoea and dirtied his spare set of clothes. As a result, he flew to Sydney in only a nappy and a hoodie.

I think the best thing is to not expect more from the kids than you do at home. Be relaxed and go with the flow as things are not always going to be perfect and at some point you are going to end up sitting on your luggage waiting (if your luggage has turned up at the right airport)—it's all just part of the adventure.

Natasha Key, mum of three

In-flight food and entertainment

Most budget airlines don't supply free food or activities for the kids. They run a paid food service where you can hand over your credit card and pay ridiculous amounts of money for junk food (or alcohol). So make sure you pack your own food and water supplies even if it's only an hour-long flight. One of our flights to Sydney took four and a half hours door to door as a result of delays. The kids were starving by the time we arrived and their behaviour was reflecting this.

I also make each child an activity pack when we fly. They were gold for passing the time while we waited for our flights in the departure lounges, as well as on board. Open-ended, low-mess activity packs containing items that allowed them to use their imagination—such as stickers, writing paper and envelopes—were a big hit with the four and six year old. I'd taught the older boys the basics of Blackjack (no gambling, of course). It's a fantastic card game for the kids' mental maths and can be played in a confined space.

Luggage

One airline didn't even have tags available for labelling luggage at the check-in, so make sure you have your luggage labelled. Almost all budget fares only include carry-on luggage with restrictions. At both Melbourne and Sydney they weighed the carry-on luggage and people had to remove items to get their weight down. Make sure you weigh your carry-on luggage to prevent unnecessary delays.

We purchased extra luggage and, with the tight weight restriction, I have to admit that was my best-ever packing effort.

Airports

Depending on the airline you're flying with and the city you're flying from, the departure lounge of a budget airline may be located away from those of other domestic airlines. The one in Melbourne resembled a big, old shed and was cold in winter. To board the plane we had to walk a considerable distance outdoors on a cold early morning. I was grateful that it wasn't raining as part of the walkway is not under cover. On board, however, it was quite warm, so I definitely recommend layers for travelling.

Most budget airlines do expect passengers to walk on the tarmac to board and disembark their planes. It's part of the strategy for turning the planes around quickly by having passengers board and disembark at the front and back of the plane simultaneously. Our allocated seats were at the back of the plane each time we flew, which meant walking on the tarmac and up some very steep, steel stairs.

Despite the cold, walking on the tarmac was a highlight for our younger kids. They loved seeing how big the plane was and hearing the noises coming from other planes.

Service and amenities

Even when I travelled on my own with all five kids I received no assistance from in-flight staff. Before boarding commences, there's always an announcement calling for families and those with special needs to board first. Make sure you take advantage of this as it will give you a bit more time and space to get all the kids organised before everyone else starts to board.

Staying home with kids

I thoroughly enjoy school holidays. I love the break it gives us from the school routine, the opportunity it gives the younger kids to play with their older siblings and, as the school terms are so busy, I love the time it gives the kids to relax.

Just because I love school holidays doesn't mean that we're all happy for every moment of each day or that we're always enjoying each other's company! It certainly isn't all 'Kum ba ya' singing, peace and serenity—that's for sure. There can be major fights between kids, I can lose my patience and the house can end up looking like a bomb zone. However, with some forethought and planning as a family, we generally have a pretty good time over the school holidays.

Planning for the school holidays

Due to my enthusiasm for giving the kids some fun experiences and catching up with friends, I've often made the mistake of over scheduling our school holidays. It's amazing how quickly you can end up with something planned every single day. The end result is that the kids and I go back to school feeling even more tired. To prevent this from happening, I created a school holiday plan with the kids.

Kids don't need to be bombarded with plays and outings in the holidays. Let them chill out, turn off the TV and encourage children to play with their siblings and create their own fun.

Alison Sexton, mum of four

At a family meeting in the lead-up to school holidays, I ask the kids whether there's anything special they'd like to do during the holidays. Each child is allowed to choose one activity. We agree on the activities and then I schedule them at intervals—where possible—so we have a mix of days at home and days out. I aim to schedule in a day or two at home at the beginning of the holidays (so everyone can get some rest after the long school term) and then some days at home again towards the end of the holidays (so that the kids head back to school refreshed).

Leading up to school holidays we have a list on the fridge so the children can write on the list what they would like to do—you would be surprised what they write. An outing to the local café is always on top of the list.

Georgina Rechner, mum of three

Table 12.6 illustrates what a plan for our September school holidays may look like. You can find a template for the school holiday plan at <www.planningwithkids.com/resources>.

Table 12.6: school holiday plan

	Mon.	Tues.	Wed.	Thurs.	Fri.	Sat.	Sun.
Week 1	Home	A day with friends	Collingwood F.C. training session	Home	Healesville Sanctuary	AFL Grand Final party	Home
Week 2	Pool with friends	Café lunch with friends	Home	Home	Home	Shopping	Home

It's important for us to have time away from the house. If we stay home for too many days in a row, we tend to end up with cabin fever. The changes of scenery help make sure that we're all still getting along harmoniously.

Tip

Preparing for the school holidays

These tips are aimed at having things organised around the house before the school holidays start. My favourite part about school holidays is that there's less running around. I find it incredibly helpful to stock up on necessary supplies before the holidays to minimise the number of trips to the shopping centre during school holidays.

Stocking up on cooking supplies

This has two purposes. First, with all of the kids home and catch-ups with friends, we tend to go through a lot of food. Second, my kids love to cook for fun during the school holidays.

Stocking up on lunch and morning-tea ingredients

During the school holidays it used to feel like all I did was prepare food and tidy up afterwards! So I started getting the kids to be responsible for doing some of this themselves. Now, they alternate making morning tea among themselves and I alternate preparing lunch with them. To make this easy for the younger children I ensure I have plenty of food supplies on hand so they can prepare morning tea and lunch easily on their own.

Stocking up on craft and art supplies

These don't need to be expensive. We keep it pretty simple by collecting boxes and cartons in the weeks leading up to the holidays (these are great materials for the kids to build

Preparing for the school holidays (*cont'd*)

things with). The craft and art supplies I like to make sure
I have on hand are:

▷ drawing paper and card

▷ recycled boxes

▷ straws

▷ paper plates and cups

▷ masking tape

▷ staples

▷ glue (glue sticks, craft glue and refills for the hot
glue gun)

▷ chalk

▷ string

▷ beads

▷ Blu-Tack

▷ pegs.

Home activities

There are endless possibilities in terms of how to entertain
the kids at home during the holidays. I've found that with
my kids it's having simple activities where they're in control
that they enjoy the most. Here are a few things you might
like to try doing at home:

- make lemonade
- cook the kids' favourite treats with them
- paint a canvas together
- play musical statues
- make a bird feeder
- play indoor or outdoor hide-and-seek

- brighten up the pavement with some chalk drawing
- make a volcano
- make a giant cardboard construction
- do some gardening
- camp inside or outside at home (depending on the weather)
- have a water-bomb fight
- make your own movie
- make a cubby house
- set up a balloon volleyball net inside
- turn the kitchen into a café and let all kids take on a role to make lunch
- invite some friends for a sleepover
- make mud pies
- play board games
- put on a puppet show
- make a LEGO city together
- go through the family photo albums
- cook up some playdough with the kids
- make up your own bubble solution
- write a funny story together, taking turns to write a sentence each
- create an obstacle course in the garden.

Local school-holiday activities

Melbourne offers a wealth of entertainment options to choose from all year round, and even more during school holidays. Some of these are generic and can be found in most towns and cities. I subscribe to newsletters from places such as galleries, community houses, public gardens, libraries and community groups so that I'm notified of upcoming events. Many free or low-cost events book out quickly, so it's great to be advised early that tickets are on sale.

Spend time doing things together, if you can get away from home. Even if it's just for a day or two, do it. Fun doesn't always need to be expensive: a day at the beach or playing in the park can be just as rewarding as a trip to the movies or [a] visit to the zoo and they're both free.

Stephen Fulton, dad of three

Here are some low-cost ideas for having fun with the kids away from home. While some are only available during school holidays, many can also be done year round:

- visit an art gallery
- join a local tree planting session
- visit a museum
- go for a bike ride
- go bush walking
- explore new parks in the area
- visit a community farm
- see some local live music (check out local pubs if you don't have specific live-music venues as they can often have family-friendly sessions)
- go fishing
- investigate community-house holiday programs
- hire a row boat
- take a train ride to somewhere new
- go market shopping for a family feast
- go rock climbing
- visit the beach/river/lake
- attend a local sporting event
- check out the local library's school holiday program
- attend a community festival
- visit your local botanic gardens (or similar)
- see a local drama production
- swim at the local pool
- go fruit picking.

But I'm bored!

Even with the best planning, at some point during the school holidays one of my children will come up with the 'I'm bored' call. As I've already mentioned, I think it's good for kids to get to this point, but I have to remind myself not to jump in and give them ideas on how to occupy themselves. For our nine-year-old son, it's deciding what he wants to do that's the problem. Once he's decided on something, he'll stick at it for a long time, but it can often take him a while and a fair bit of whining to find the right activity.

Frustrated by this pattern of behaviour, during one school-holiday break I sat down with him and made him write a list of things he liked to do. A couple of his siblings sat with us and helped us build a comprehensive list. His first task was to type up his list on the computer and print it out (which kept him from being 'bored' for a while). He stuck it on the notice board and it became a reference point for him.

After that, I'd see him check his list regularly during the holidays and then wander off to start something new. If he needed materials he'd come to me for assistance, but he no longer came to me whining that he didn't have anything to do! This is what his list looked like:

- wrestling
- soccer games (outside)
- kick a ball against the wall
- go for a run
- play balloon games inside (balloon volleyball, keepies off)
- listen to a Harry Potter audio book
- play chess
- read a book
- ride my bike
- play in the park next door

- build some LEGO
- construct something with a glue gun
- play a board game (Mastermind, Scrabble, Boggle, Monopoly)
- write a story/letter/email
- create an experiment or a potion
- listen to my iPod
- do some gardening
- do some cooking
- do a puzzle
- practise batting with the cricket wiz
- unscrew an old appliance (one no longer in use)
- climb a tree
- build a fort.

Seeing this list up on the notice board made our four year old decide he needed one too. We created a picture list together with less choice than the one for our nine year old. Too many options can be overwhelming and cause indecision for a four year old. As he wasn't at school yet, he referred to this list all the time. This is what his list looked like:

- noughts and crosses
- puzzles
- LEGO
- play with hot wheels action sets
- trampoline
- pavement chalk drawing
- scooter.

Downloadable templates of the boredom-buster lists can be found at <www.planningwithkids.com/resources>.

Taking action

- Take time to prepare the house before you go on holidays so it's secure and in an organised state when you return.

- Make packing for a family holiday easier and more efficient by creating checklists that involve the whole family's participation.

- Create activity packs to entertain the kids as you travel.

- Proactively manage the car trip with the kids so the journey itself is part of the fun.

- If you're flying with budget airlines, ensure you prepare in advance and are ready for possible delays.

- When staying at home for school holidays, create a school-holiday plan to balance out activities for the kids and yourself.

- In the week leading up to the school holidays, stock up on essentials so you have plenty of food and craft supplies for the kids.

- Get kids who find it difficult to start on activities on their own to write up a list of activities at the beginning of the holidays as a reference guide.

Chapter 13

Stress-free birthday parties

I love kids' birthday parties. I have fond memories of my own and going to my friends' houses for parties as a child. In recent years there's been a growing trend towards outsourcing kids' parties. While these types of parties are lots of fun, they don't always suit our family budget or philosophy. We usually choose to stay with the traditional home birthday party.

The thought of having 15 kids ready to party on your doorstep can be a little terrifying, but with some planning I've been able to keep within the family budget and spread out the work involved so it's enjoyable for the kids and doesn't drive me insane!

Planning a stay-at-home party

When planning a kid's birthday party I find the simplest option is usually the best. To streamline the party organisation and keep it simple, I use a 10-point birthday party plan. A 10-point plan might sound complex and work-heavy, but all it does is define the work involved and put it into manageable chunks. Part of the fear of organising a party can be not knowing where to start. This 10-step plan tells you where to start and what to do next. You need to prepare:

- an overall family birthday party strategy
- a party theme
- the invitations
- the guest list
- the food and drinks list
- a games or activities plan
- the lolly/treat bags
- your party week and party day work schedules
- an emergency plan
- thank-you cards.

The 10-step birthday party plan checklist can be downloaded from <www.planningwithkids.com/resources>.

Step 1: Overall family birthday party strategy

Two of our children have birthdays within 10 days of each other in April. The remaining three are at the other end of the year, with one at the end of November, one in mid December and our youngest child's birthday after Christmas. It's been jibed at me that for someone who loves to plan I didn't do such a great job of planning my children's arrivals in this world. There are some things that you just can't plan!

> *Only celebrate big birthdays with a party (5, 10, 13, 18, 21 and so on). It's okay to have a couple of friends over for a sleep-over in between, but the significance of special occasions are lost if a party is expected every year.*
>
> Stephen Fulton, dad to three

Prior to the birth of our fourth child I realised that the way we'd been celebrating birthdays was not sustainable. Being such an enthusiastic mum and wanting parity for the younger children, I'd created an expectation in my kids that they'd have a big party every year. Every year that I gave each child a party I reinforced the expectation. Having a large party every year was not only too expensive for us, but due to the clustering of the kids' actual birthdays, it was physically exhausting for me to have to prepare multiple parties.

My husband and I decided to bring the issue of birthday parties up at a family meeting. We gave the kids prior notice that we'd be discussing parties and asked them to think about how we could celebrate birthdays in the future. With input from the kids, we managed to come up with a solution everyone was happy with. The older boys both thought that having a party every second year would be a good idea, so this formed the basis for the birthday-party rotation strategy shown in table 13.1: one year they would have a small celebration, followed the next year by a home-based party. For example, in the year when one of the April children and the early December child have a party, the other two have a small celebration.

> *Alternate: one year a party and the next a great present. This helps the parties to be kept special.*
>
> Julie Holden, mum of two

Table 13.1: birthday party rotation

Small celebration	Party
Child gets to choose the dinner (home cooked or take away) on the night of their birthday or the closest Friday night	Home-based party
Child chooses two friends to come for dinner	10–15 friends
Child chooses the type of home-made birthday cake they would like	Child chooses the theme for their party (for example, sport, construction, beading)
Child chooses a DVD to watch after dinner	Child chooses the type of homemade birthday cake and food they would like
Mum or Dad drive their friends home	Homemade activities and entertainment

Now all the kids are clear about what they can expect each year for their birthday. From my perspective, it's smoothed out my birthday party workload and reduced our costs. As the children get older and move on to secondary school we'll review it again to make sure we continue to have suitable ways of celebrating birthdays.

Step 2: Party theme

Once you've chosen a theme, other decisions such as games, the food and the cake become easier because you can align them to the theme. I recommend keeping the theme simple, and if you want to keep the costs down I also recommend avoiding 'branded' themes. You can easily address a child's interest with a generic equivalent, for example:

- Bob the Builder → construction
- Thomas the Tank Engine → trains
- Hannah Montana → singing and dancing.

In table 13.2 I've listed themes that we've used in the past, or themes from great parties that we've attended to give you some inspiration. Themes are listed by age group: some can cross over multiple age groups and some themes could be used for all ages.

Table 13.2: birthday party themes

For toddlers (0–3)	For preschoolers (4–5)	For children in lower-primary school (6–9)
Favourite colour/s (for example, pink; blue and silver; primary colours)	Pirates	Sports parties (for example, cricket; football; netball; athletics)
Favourite animal	Knights	Jewellery-making
Favourite nursery rhyme	Dinosaurs	Card-making
Sand play	Trains	Construction (wooden kits; cardboard boxes)
Water play – luau	Princess/ fairies	Science experiments (potion making)
Cars or any big machinery	Butterflies	Karaoke
Construction (blocks, hammering, recycled materials)	Hearts	Cooking
Music (home-made shakers, drums, etc.)	Garden tea party	Photography

Step 3: Invitations

You can create a very simple invitation at home that's inexpensive and involves the kids. Some styles we use frequently are:

- photo-based:
  - Use a recent photo as a centrepiece of the invitation.
  - Attach it to coloured card and write the party details on the back.
  - Decorate it with items that reflect the theme—for example, pink dots. Depending on the age of the child, they can help do this. (I try to keep the children involved as much as possible in the party preparations.)

- theme-designed:
  - Make the base shape of the invitation fit the theme (for example, a football, shield, rocket, crown).
  - Use colours and wording to fit the theme.
  - Type the party details into a space that can be stuck onto the card.
  - Print out and attach this to the base shape.

- child-designed:
  - Have the child draw a picture in Tux, Paint or another computer drawing application. (Paint can be found under Accessories in the Start menu of Microsoft.)
  - Insert the picture and add your words to a Word document.

- Print this out and let the child cut out the design.

- Paste it to coloured card.

- Older children can use more advanced programs such as PowerPoint to design their own invitation on the computer and print it out for their friends.

Step 4: Guest list

Once we've decided who we're inviting, I type a list of names into a spreadsheet (although this could also be a handwritten list). I then stick a copy of the list on the wall near the phone. That way, if anyone takes an RSVP call about the party, they can easily mark the response on the sheet.

Step 5: Food and drinks list

One of the reasons I keep a guest list in spreadsheet form is so I can use the numbers to calculate the quantities of foods we'll need. I create a food and drink list linked to the number of adults and kids who'll be attending. Then I can quickly determine the exact food requirements for the party. I'm notorious for over-catering, so having a list to refer to for quantities helps give me perspective. I can also quickly work out by how much I need to multiply my recipes to work out how much food we need, which makes shopping easier too. Table 13.3 shows an example of a food and drinks list.

You can download a template for the food and drinks list at <www.planningwithkids.com/resources>.

Aligning the food with the party theme also makes decisions about what to serve a bit easier. Here are some food (and set-up) ideas we've used for themed birthday parties.

Table 13.3: food and drinks

Food	Number for all to share	Pieces per child (11)	Pieces per adult (7)	Total quantity
Starters				
Turkish bread and dips	2			**2**
Chocolate balls		3	3	**54**
Teacup biscuits		2	1	**29**
Pineapple boats	2			**2**
Kiwi-fruit cocktail		1	0	**11**
Lunch				
Shaped sandwiches		2	1	**29**
Mini pizzas		2	1	**29**
Chicken wings		3	3	**54**
Afters				
Frozen banana ice-creams		1	0	**11**
End				
Birthday cake	1			**1**

- Knight theme — a long banquet table:

    — set up a long trestle as a banquet table

    — serve chicken wings and drumsticks, baked potatoes, corn on the cob and chunks of bread as the main food

    — use goblet-shaped cups for the children to drink from

    — make a lamington castle cake with lamingtons stacked like bricks, complete with turrets.

- Football theme — individual snack boxes:

    — cut up oranges

- make or buy cheap snack boxes (I used cardboard meal boxes)
- pack a hot dog, two meat pies, two sausage rolls, a serviette and a fruit juice into each meal box
- add a few chocolate balls and a small chocolate mud cake to each meal box
- sit outside on picnic blankets
- bake a rectangular cake that looks like a football pitch, complete with little plastic football players.

• Water party theme—luau:
- set up a low, long table that children can sit around
- provide lots of fruit-based foods such as pineapple boats, fruit skewers and kiwi-fruit cocktails
- make flower-shaped sandwiches, mini Hawaiian pizzas and chicken wings
- make chocolate balls and roll them in coconut dyed pink and yellow using food colouring
- make frozen banana ice-creams
- serve a homemade berry ice-cream cake.

• Garden tea party:
- set up a table and chairs outside; decorate the table with rose petals and leaves
- use real china teacups, a teapot and sandwich plates
- bake fairy cakes, teacup biscuits and sprinkled (hundreds and thousands) biscuits

- make sandwiches cut into fingers and filled with chicken, cucumber and cheese; and ham and cheese

- finish off with a cinnamon tea cake decorated with flowers.

A great tip for serving food at a kid's party is to use snack boxes. Party-supply places usually sell these very cheaply. We've used rectangular cardboard boxes (like the ones used for fish and chips), which cost about 12 cents each.

We then spread out blankets either inside or outside (depending on the weather) and all the children sit together to eat. Kids will sit calmly for 10 to 15 minutes eating and chatting. There's much less wastage as kids actually eat the food because they're all seated. Tidying up is also incredibly easy. Scraps make their way to the rubbish bin and the snack boxes can be put into the recycling bin. The blankets help keep all the crumbs off the floor, which means less cleaning up for me.

Step 6: Games or activities plan

Children are very adept at creating their own fun, so for parties I like to have a mix of structured activities and time for the kids to just play. The activities and play differ for each age group and the type of party we have.

One-to-three years old

For this age group, I prepare an area where the children can play freely. I've found that organising games for this age doesn't work well as they're still finding the concept of sharing and turn-taking pretty difficult. Given age-appropriate toys and props, children this age will explore, play and entertain themselves quite easily. Adults need only to keep a watch on proceedings and lead with examples of play ideas if the toddlers are unsure of what to do.

For a three year old's construction party we had the following materials set up for the kids:

- a box containing recycled materials, masking tape, string and staplers with which they could make a creation using their imagination

- real small-sized hammers, and nails (clouts, as they have bigger heads)

- chalk for drawing on the pavement

- buckets and paint brushes for water painting.

For the water-themed party for a two year old we set up:

- two little blow-up pools full of water and water-play toys such as funnels, jugs, scoops and buckets

- two child-sized tables set up with tea sets for those children who didn't want to get into the pools but were happy to play with the water

- child-sized watering cans, so those who wanted to could walk around the garden and water the plants.

For a one-year-old primary-coloured theme party we:

- moved all the furniture to the sides of one room

- had primary-coloured helium balloons tied to decorative weights around the room; the balloons are a natural draw card for little ones

- provided toys such as mega blocks, little people, a tea set and balls and placed them in different corners of the room.

Four-to-six years old

This age group is able to participate more cooperatively in games and activities, but a combination of free play and structured activities works best to ensure the party remains calm and happy. Lots of high-energy boys and girls left to their own devices for too long can cause a little bit of mayhem! Here are some games we've played at a football-themed party.

- Upon arrival, each child was asked to write their name and a number on a new T-shirt with fabric crayons. We had bought three different coloured T-shirts, so the children could easily recognise which team they were in. We then ironed the print, which we covered with a cloth, and this became their team T-shirt for the games and also their take-home gift.

- We played a round robin of 15-minute soccer games.

- Orange breaks: as the kids play very hard, those who were sitting out and watching the others play ate oranges and drank water to refresh themselves.

- We also had penalty shoot-outs where the kids competed against my husband as the goalie!

Seven-to-nine years old

At this age—depending on the number of children—you can set the children up with a comprehensive activity aligned with the party theme. At a jewellery party for a seven year old, for example, the kids could make a collection of basic pieces to take home with them, such as:

- a braided wristband

- a lolly necklace

- a beaded bracelet.

Step 7: Lolly/treat bags

The type of lolly bag that we prepare for the partygoers depends on their age.

Kids under three

I try to avoid confectionery, so for this age I find cute little boxes, bags or tins that can be used as take-home gifts and I place small treats in them, such as tiny teddies, toddler fruitbars or homemade cookies.

Kids over three

By this age I can no longer get away with a healthy treat bag so I allow the kids to make some decisions about what they'd like in their lolly bags. I try to encourage them to include a small theme-aligned trinket and only a few lollies.

You can use either brown paper bags or small cardboard noodle boxes to put the lollies in. This is a great way to have children involved in preparing for their party. The children can help decorate the boxes or bags using the party's theme for inspiration. The night before the party I let them fill the bags or boxes themselves—after showing them an orderly process for doing this—and they love it.

Step 8: Party week and party day work schedules

Having a work plan helps me make decisions about such things as the type of food I'll serve. If I need to make some of the food the night before, I may choose an ice-cream cake, which can be made in advance. This means I don't have too many things to do the night before or the day of the party.

We almost always have home-made ice-cream cakes at our home parties. They are easy to make and customise with the birthday child's favourite ingredients. By scooping into cones to serve, there are no plates to wash up and far fewer crumbs!! You do have to make sure there's enough for the adults too!!

Cath Taylor, mum of three <www.mobblegobble.com>

Party week schedule

About a week before the party, I write down everything I need to do over the coming days and I spread the tasks out so that all the work isn't left to the day before the party. This prevents a repeat performance of times when I left everything to the last minute and ended up going to bed at 2 am on the day of the party. Just having the list makes me feel more organised as I know what I need to do and when. Table 13.4 is a list of what and when things had to be done for our two-year-old daughter's water/luau-themed party.

Table 13.4: party week schedule

Task	When to do it!
Buy pool-fixing tape	Wed — on the way to kindy gym
General shopping	Wed — during kindy gym and remainder in the evening
Make cake	Wed night
Make chocolate balls	Wed night
Make teacups	Thu morning
Bathers for daughter	Thu during kindy gym
Buy Elvis Hawaii music	Thu during kindy gym
Buy chicken wings	Thu after school drop-off

Table 13.4 (*cont'd*): party week schedule

Task	When to do it!
Buy fruit	Thu after school drop-off
Clean house	Thu night
Lolly bags	Thu night
Make banana ice-creams	Thu night
Wrap birthday girl's present	Thu night
Buy Turkish bread and sandwich bread	Fri morning
Get ingredients ready for little pizzas	Fri morning
Make pineapple boats	Fri morning
Make sandwiches	Fri morning
Puree kiwi fruit	Fri morning
Set up food table	Fri morning
Set up pools	Fri morning

You can find a template for my party week schedule at <www.planningwithkids.com/resources>.

Party day timetable

The party day timetable is really just for me. I enjoy it when our birthday parties are relatively free-flowing for the kids, especially the little ones who are not old enough for structured games. If things are flowing smoothly and the kids want to stick with whatever they're doing, I allow myself to be led by the mood on the day of the party. By breaking down the party preparation into discrete tasks, I have a clear idea of the work that needs to be done and when. I find this particularly useful if I'm serving hot food and it all has to be ready at the same time.

Another advantage of having a timetable is that if you're lucky enough to have some adult helpers they refer to this list of tasks if they want to help out. My sisters and close friends have always been fabulous at helping out on the day of our kids' parties. Having the list—which you can see in table 13.5—means that while I'm outside playing with the kids one of my lovely sisters can do things such as putting the pizzas on at the right time and keeping an eye on them so they'll be ready in time for lunch.

Table 13.5: party day timing

Time	Activity
5.50 am	Mum: shower
6.15 am	Make school lunchbox
6.30 am	Make sandwiches
6.50 am	Make mini pizzas
7.00 am	Dad: set up table
7.15 am	Make pineapple boats
7.50 am	Make kiwi puree
8.00 am	Organise children
8.10 am	Tidy house
8.20 am	Drop big kids at school and buy bread
8.45 am	Continue tidying house
9.45 am	Set up pools and turn on oven
10.00 am	Start to cook chicken wings

Table 13.5 (*cont'd*): party day timing

Time	Activity
10.30 am	Party starts: guests arrive—hand out leis
10.30 am	Play with water and tea sets
10.50 am	Cook mini pizzas
11.10 am	Serve lunch, including drinks
11.30 am	Serve banana ice-creams
11.40 am	Play with water and tea sets
12.15 pm	Serve birthday cake
12.30 pm	Party finishes: hand out lolly bags

You can find a template for my party day timetable at <www.planningwithkids.com/resources>.

Step 9: Emergency plan

It's wise to have a Plan B if you're having a party at home that involves outdoor activities. Plan B can be very simple and low-cost. Games such as musical statues, balloons and box construction can all be great standby activities should the weather turn inclement.

One year we had a football party planned for our six-year-old boy. It ended up pouring with rain half an hour before the party was due to start. It continued to pour rain for pretty much the whole party. Luckily, kids are nowhere near as fickle as adults about a little thing like rain so, with Dad out there refereeing, the game went on. (Well, for 40 minutes at least, until the referee decided that was enough!)

Plan A had been to play round robin games of football, have lunch, play soccer-skills games, eat cake and go home. We'd checked out the forecast and could see rain on the horizon so Plan B was football, musical statues (I downloaded the top 40 songs under direction from the kids, which they said were the songs that 'everyone at school liked', even though they weren't to my taste!), lunch, inside balloon games (teams keeping the balloon off the ground and popping a balloon to receive a lolly), eat cake and go home.

When the rain became too heavy for the kids to play in, I was so relieved to have a Plan B and the resources to implement it. With 18 seven-year-old boys in the house, it could have otherwise ended up a bit wild.

Step 10: Thank-you cards

I started sending out thank-you notes for children's birthday parties when we moved to Surrey Hills. It wasn't the norm among my inner-city friends to do this, but in the eastern suburbs it appeared to be, and I like the idea of the children acknowledging and being grateful for the gifts they received.

The thank-you cards can be very simple, using a similar design to the invitation. Or, it can be a group photo of the party with a 'thank you' written on the back by you or your child.

Parties away from home

As much as I love traditional at-home parties (which is how we normally celebrate birthdays), there have been times when we've chosen different options. When we were living in the inner city, we had a courtyard the size of a car-parking space and our house was quite small. When my eldest son turned four it was no longer possible to have a party at home—there just wasn't enough room for all the kids we wanted to invite. When he turned four we had his dinosaur party at a local park, which was ideal for his age group.

On his sixth birthday we were in the process of looking for a new house. We'd sold our house and were running out of time to buy a new one. Most of my time was spent house hunting and there wasn't time for me to think about—let alone organise—a party at home, or even in a park. That year we completely outsourced his birthday party. We went to a local pool that catered for parties and it was the first time we too only had to turn up for our own child's party.

The outsourced pool party was the most expensive party we've ever had, but it was the best option for us at the time. For me, parties are supposed to be fun. If putting the party together is a stressful undertaking, then I reconsider my options. If, even after you've read the 10-point birthday plan, you still think the home-party idea is not for you—you may not have the space, or have too much going on—here are some middle-ground options between a home party and an outsourced party you could consider.

Picnic in the park

If the kids are under four, find a park with an enclosed play area and toilets close by—it makes the party less stressful. Use picnic blankets for the children to sit on when it's time to eat. Take along a stash of nappy wipes, your own rubbish bags and sunscreen—you'll almost always need them.

The movie theatre

Movies can be pretty expensive, so if you choose a movie party, invite fewer kids. Take along your own party-style food as the food at the movies is always overpriced.

A local activity

One year when we had a newborn, my husband and one of his friends took the kids rock climbing for two hours. Then they came home for party food and birthday cake.

Combined party in a local hall

I have friends whose kids' birthdays are close together and who have many mutual friends, so they host combined birthday parties. They split the hire of a local hall and share the catering. They bring along toys (or hire a party pack from a toy library) and let the kids play. This works well for winter parties, when the weather can be unreliable.

Birthday presents

I'm one of those people who frequently buy books as birthday presents. I think they make great gifts. However, it doesn't seem appropriate to give the same child a book for a present year after year. I prefer to stay away from commercially oriented gifts, but I do like to keep the price under $20. We keep a list of ideas for inspiration, which is helpful when the younger children who want to have a say in the gift have to choose something but can't actually think of anything! Table 13.6 (overleaf) lists some presents we've given or received over the years.

Commence [writing] a list of all family and friends and new arrivals for the year and buy gifts as you see items on sale. Write notes in [a] diary/notebook to keep track of what you have collected.

Kyrstie Barcak, mum of two

Table 13.6: birthday presents

Item	Description	Age
Little cook's set	You can purchase these from a large retail chain's kitchen-utensils section or from discount stores: a small grater, a pair of small tongs, a small whisk, a small ladle and a small sifter. I wrap them up in a colourful children's apron or tea towel to make a little cook's set.	1–3
Photo story book	This one takes some planning, and it's something I like to do for my nephews and the kids of close friends, whom I see frequently. In the few months leading up to their birthday, I inconspicuously take photos of the child on their own, with my kids and with their mum/dad/siblings, doing their favourite things; or of any other important events in their life. I then choose the best 10 or 12 photos and compile them into a photo book. I get my children to help write a little story connecting the photos and then create a cardboard front and back page. The birthday child is then the star of their very own story.	1–3
Toolbox	Buy a small tool box and add a small (real) hammer, nails (clouts are best) and — if you can get your hands on one — a piece of old weathered tree stump. It's perfect softwood for youngsters to practise on.	3–6
Black and metallic kit	This is a home-style packaged gift as well. I buy a notepad/s of black paper as well as metallic crayons and metallic coloured pencils. Then I buy a large pencil case to place everything into.	3–6

Item	Description	Age
Design-your-own T-shirt	I buy a plain white T-shirt that will fit the birthday child, and some fabric crayons. The child then designs their own T-shirt, by drawing on it with the fabric crayons. Then I iron the print, which I cover with a cloth, and the design becomes permanent.	4–8
Outdoor kit	These are great ideas for kids whose families are active outdoors. I combine a child-sized, foldable chair with a small, hand-held torch. Even if the family doesn't venture too far from their own backyard, kids love having their 'own' things to use at a barbecue or party.	4–8

Taking action

• Decide how your family will celebrate birthdays and, if possible, involve the kids in the decision making.

• Create a work plan to manage preparation for the birthday party.

• Create a plan to manage the things you have to do in the days leading up to and on the day of the party.

• Remember that birthday parties are meant to be fun and that planning is a way of making them hassle-free so that you can have fun too!

• Choose a style of birthday party that your child and family will enjoy at the time (home, outdoor or outsourced, for example).

• Create a list of favourite presents to use as a reference for you and the kids when you have to buy a gift.

Chapter 14

Avoiding
Christmas chaos

Christmas can be an incredibly hectic time in the southern hemisphere because it coincides with the end of the school year. Add two kids' birthdays in the lead-up to Christmas and, if I don't start getting my head around Christmas before November, I find myself very stressed and exhausted by the end of the year. To help smooth out the Christmas workload I break my Christmas into two parts. The first is Christmas preparation in July, and the second is having a 10-week Christmas preparation plan for the weeks leading up to Christmas.

Christmas preparation in July

Over the past couple of years I've started doing some initial planning for Christmas in July, and this has helped me stay sane and get some sleep in the lead-up to Christmas. Previously, without kick starting my Christmas planning in July, at times December look a bit like this:

- I decide I want to handmake gifts for the kids' teachers. I choose a simple craft item, which inevitably takes longer to make than I anticipated. The kids are too tired to help (or I don't have the patience to let them help). For several nights I'm up until after 11 pm finishing said craft items.

- I frantically finish writing all the Christmas cards in the remaining days before Christmas, crossing my fingers that they'll make it to their destination before the big day.

- I make the dreaded trip to a large shopping centre along with more than half of the population of Melbourne on the final Saturday before Christmas to complete the present shopping.

Christmas: the where, when and who

My parents and much of our extended family live in Mildura. For the past 10 years or so, we've alternated between spending Christmas in Mildura or Melbourne. There are years, though, when — due to various circumstances — this changes. Having babies, attending weddings and availability of family all need to be considered when working out where we're going to spend Christmas. Determining where we'll be and who's hosting Christmas in July gives me more time to meet my responsibilities and get our family organised.

Father Christmas brings to all in our family. The children write lists, so we know what each other would like. All the gifts are laid carefully out on the floor, everyone knows who the LEGO is for, and the size-10 roller blades but by not putting it in the sack it is assumed everything is to be shared and does not belong to one alone.

Georgina Rechner, mum of three

Choosing a theme for Christmas

A recent addition to my Christmas preparation has been to choose a theme for Christmas. I have friends who've been doing this for a number of years and my friend Justine in particular showed me how well it can work. For example, it:

- makes the decision-making process in relation to necessities such as cards, decorations and wrappings much easier

- simplifies the choice of Christmas accessories you make/buy for the house

- allows a simple and coordinated look for your Christmas celebrations

- can help guide the menu for the big day

- adds to the memory ('It was the "gold" Christmas!').

The theme can be very simple, such as choosing colours (red and white), or it can incorporate a motif such as birds or angels. I have friends who choose a theme right after Christmas for the next one and take advantage of the discounted prices on Christmas decorations. I don't buy new decorations every year as that would not fit in our budget, but I do make simple, inexpensive decorations to go with the theme. For example, if you choose a natural theme early in the year, when winter comes you can start collecting things such as pine cones and acorns—free natural materials that you can turn into decorations. You may like to consider the themes described below for your next Christmas.

A natural look

- Use pine cones to make a wreath.

- Cinnamon sticks can be used as tree decorations— instructions can be found at <www.planningwithkids. com/2010/11/18/natural-christmas-decorations>.

- Try brown recycled paper and twine for gift-wrapping.
- Use dried branches decorated with baubles as a table centrepiece.

Red and white

- Buy a traditional, basic wreath and add red and white ribbons to it—instructions can be found at <www.maxabellaloves.blogspot.com/2010/12/loving-christmas-spirit.html>.

- Using red and white patterned paper, make doves to hang on the Christmas tree—instructions can be found at <www.keepcatebusy.blogspot.com/2010/12/day-66-hooray-for-inspiration.html>.

- Try combinations of red and white stripes and red and white dots for wrapping gifts.

- Fill white bowls with candy canes for table decorations.

Blue and silver

- Make a blue-and-silver bauble wreath—instructions can be found at <www.homelife.com.au/home+ideas/decorating/how+to+make+your+own+christmas+door+wreath,3592>.

- Make gorgeous glittery string baubles—instructions can be found at <www.marthastewart.com/article/snowy-ornaments>.

- Alternate blue and silver paper with silver and blue ribbon when wrapping gifts.

- Put floating candles into shallow blue bowls to use as table decorations.

Non-traditional bright colours (pink, blue, green, yellow, orange)

- A button wreath made from scraps of fabric is easy to put together with the kids—instructions can be found at <www.jackobindi.blogspot.com/2009/11/make-fabric-button-christmas-wreath.html>.

- Make funky paper baubles for tree decorations—instructions can be found at <www.homemade-gifts-made-easy.com/christmas-ornaments-to-make.html>.

- Plain, brightly coloured paper with thick clashing ribbon is great for wrapping gifts.

- Try tall glass vases filled with brightly coloured baubles as table decorations.

Handmade Christmas gifts

For me, there's something special about receiving a gift that someone has spent their time creating especially for you. I'm not a great sewer or crafter, but I do like to make simple things on my own and with the kids to give to people for Christmas. My dear friend Cath, however, is very good at craft, but not so much of a planner. Over the past couple of years we've combined our skills to start making handmade gifts in the middle of the year.

I teach my kids it is about giving and being together, not about getting what you want.

Stephen Fulton, dad of three

Cath and I start with a planning meeting where we find ideas and choose a number of them to make. We then meet every few weeks in the evening and work on the projects together. This is more for my benefit, so Cath can show me how it's all done. I also make simpler craft items with the kids. It's great for them to be involved in making the gifts they'll be giving to their teachers and other important people in their life. By the time November comes we've handmade a pile of gifts for friends and family.

With the proliferation of craft blogs on the internet, there's no shortage of ideas and inspiration for simple, handmade projects. Now if you're thinking, 'I'm not craft-minded' and plan to skip over the list, you should know that if I can make these, anyone can! There is no sewing required, and children can make most of the items with assistance. So try them out by following the easy tutorials at <www.planningwithkids. com/resources>.

Some handmade Christmas gift ideas include:

- fabric-covered notebooks
- bath salts
- fabric-covered stationery
- coasters
- hair ties
- chocolate sauce
- chalkboard notice boards
- tea for one
- cinnamon sticks
- rocky road gift packs.

[Our] milkshake maker continues to be as popular as our popcorn maker and they are great gifts for families! Magazine subscriptions work well for those tricky teenagers; my nephew

loves all things IT—so I renew his subscription to Australian PC *each year. My niece loves* Dolly—*so the same for her. My mum gives 'family passes' to events or places each year, for example, Healesville Sanctuary, zoo, Puffing Billy and the like!*

Carolyn Ratnik, mum of three

A 10-week Christmas preparation plan

I've mentioned before how one of my favourite aspects of planning is that once you've detailed a plan you can run on autopilot, just checking in on the plan to tick off a completed task and look at the next one. For me, this works particularly well in the lead-up to Christmas. With so many functions to attend and preparations to organise, I can have my 10-week plan stuck prominently on the front of the fridge and work my way steadily through the list and not feel out of control.

We put up an advent calendar every year at Christmas. The children put it together. Each day has a surprise. Ideas are 'choose a DVD', 'decide on dinner or dessert', or 'have a special outing'.

Katie McIntosh, mum of eight

Not everything that has to be done is written in the plan, but the main tasks are all included. By following the plan, I can balance my workload evenly instead of enduring the mad last-minute rush of some previous Christmases. The plan also provides flexibility. I can rearrange the order of tasks for most weeks, depending on what comes up family-wise during a particular week. For example, if the kids are sick in the week I planned to make the Christmas cards with them, I can make the Christmas tags instead. Table 14.1 gives an example of a 10-week Christmas plan.

Table 14.1: a 10-week Christmas plan

Time before Christmas	Task	Notes
10 weeks	Review Christmas budget	We have a fixed amount of money available to spend on Christmas. I track expenditure via a spreadsheet to make sure I don't overspend. You can find a Christmas planning master spreadsheet at <www.planningwithkids.com/resources> that incorporates the Christmas budget and other lists I refer to in the plan.
9 weeks	Finish handmade gifts	The aim is to have them completed before I start birthday celebrations for my eldest son at the end of November.
8 weeks	Update Christmas card list and start making family Christmas cards	Add, delete and amend as necessary! If you don't make your own cards, this is still a good time to buy Christmas cards so you have plenty of time to write them.
7 weeks	Help kids make children's cards and continue writing family cards	Some of our kids like to make their own cards each year (using a similar process as outlined for invitations). As they handwrite their greetings, they need plenty of time to complete them so they don't have to do all the writing in one go.
6 weeks	Finish gift tags and organise wrapping paper	I make simple gift tags and have found it easier to look for matching paper earlier rather than later. You can find instructions on how make gift tags at <www.planningwithkids.com/resources>.

Table 14.1 (*cont'd*): a 10-week Christmas plan

Time before Christmas	Task	Notes
5 weeks	Christmas present list and shopping	Over the year I keep a gift ideas list and a gifts purchased list. In years where I didn't do this I sometimes forgot about gifts I'd bought, and bought more gifts than I needed!
4 weeks	Christmas decorations	As well as making the decorations I want for Christmas, our kids love to make Christmas paper chains using recycled Christmas paper from the previous year.
3 weeks	Gather toys for giving	With the impending influx of new toys and other gifts, this is a perfect opportunity to take the kids through their things and have them donate some to charity.
2 weeks	Christmas Day preparation plan	This is like the schedules I use when preparing for the children's birthday parties. It outlines all the tasks that need to be completed and I assign a date to each one. This helps spread out the remaining workload. It also incorporates creating a specific menu plan for Christmas Day.
1 week	Shortbread and Christmas treats cooking	With the kids on school holidays it's a fun way to get into the Christmas spirit.
Christmas Day	Celebration time	If I'm hosting, I use a plan for Christmas Day to help manage the logistics and the workload.

A Christmas Day menu plan

This Christmas Day Simple Menu Plan summarises a basic Christmas lunch we prepared one year. It catered for 13 adults and six kids.

Christmas Day Simple Menu

Starters:

Sun Dried Tomato and Fetta Tarts*
Chicken and Rocket Sandwiches*

Main:

Roast Chicken (Nana to bring)
Roast Duck
Roast Beef
Leg of Ham (Poppy to bring)
Easy Potato Au Gratin*
Easy Pumpkin Au Gratin*
Honey Carrots
Steamed Greens

Dessert:

Granny's Christmas Pudding
White Chocolate Cheesecake*
Honeycomb Ice-cream Cake*

With Coffee:

Christmas Reindeer Biscuits*
Mini Christmas Puddings*

---

* Recipes can be found at <www.planningwithkids.com/resources>.

When I'm hosting Christmas Day lunch at our home, I set aside time in the weeks leading up to it for making a dedicated menu plan for the big day. Planning the food in advance means you have time to play with. You can choose some foods in advance and spread out the workload. If extended family are coming over, you can also incorporate their contributions into your plan. It could be that Granny makes the Christmas pudding and Nana brings the brandy butter, and so on. Including relatives' specialties in the menu plan not only decreases your workload, but also helps to build on Christmas traditions.

Once you've decided on your menu plan, you can allocate tasks across preceding weeks. Table 14.2 shows what the cooking plan for our Christmas Day menu looked like.

Table 14.2: Christmas cooking plan

Time before Christmas	Activity
2 weeks	Order meat and poultry from butcher and organise to pick up the day before Christmas if possible.
1 week	Make a complete shopping list and purchase all items except for fresh fruit and vegetables.
	Plan and purchase alcoholic and non-alcoholic drinks to accompany the meal.
5 days	Make the tarts and freeze them in air-tight containers.
4 days	Make the honeycomb ice-cream cake.
3 days	Make the reindeer biscuits and mini puddings with the kids.
2 days	Make the white chocolate cheesecake.
1 day	Pick up meat and poultry and purchase fresh fruit and vegetables.
	Make the chicken filling for the sandwiches.

Time before Christmas	Activity
Christmas Eve	Make up potato and pumpkin au gratin.
Christmas morning (before visitors arrive)	Place meats on to cook.
	Place potato and pumpkin au gratin on to cook.
	Prepare vegetables.
	Make up chicken sandwiches and place on platter. Cover with plastic wrap and refrigerate until needed.
Christmas Day lunch	Take chicken sandwiches out of the fridge 5 minutes before serving to remove chill.
	Reheat tarts for about 15 minutes.
	Steam vegetables 15 minutes prior to serving.
	Rest meat.
	Boil water for pudding and add pudding about 45 minutes before you wish to eat it.
	Serve and enjoy!

Enjoying Christmas Day

Christmas Day is such an exciting time for kids. In my early years of parenting I tried to keep all my usual rules and routines in place on Christmas Day. This would either see me pulling my hair out—as I found it impossible to get the kids to follow their normal routines—or the little ones crying because they were unhappy about having to do things they didn't want to. Most often it was a combination of both.

Enjoying Christmas Day (*cont'd*)

Five years down the track I grew a little wiser. Christmas is one very special day of the year and, for the family to enjoy it as much as possible, I needed to relax everything a little and take a different approach to the day. Here's how we celebrate Christmas now.

Include time for resting

It's possible for us to have every weekend fully booked in the lead-up to Christmas. This takes its toll not only on me, but the kids as well. I've started booking time out on the calendar for the family before Christmas to rest and catch our breath. Running into Christmas Day being tired reduces my ability to cope with the challenges a large family celebration can—and very often does—throw my way.

Discuss Christmas Day

We have a chat with the kids a couple of days before Christmas about what's planned for the day. We talk to them about where we're going, what we're doing, who will be there and our expectations of the kids.

Allow yourself time to enjoy the day

I try to remember Christmas is a family event and allow others to help in the preparation. This is another bonus to advance planning: I can easily delegate tasks to others earlier so I know they're taken care of. As it gets closer, I can involve my husband and kids. Even if they can't help with the cooking, they can help with things such as cleaning and gift wrapping. Two jobs I always delegate to my husband are:

▷ *checking there are enough drinks.* Make sure there are enough alcoholic and non-alcoholic drinks for everyone and that we have the facilities for keeping them cool. We only have one fridge, so this generally means filling an esky with ice the night before. With the drinks out of the fridge, I have space to store more pre-prepared food.

⟫ *checking the electronics.* Make sure the video and still cameras are charged and have plenty of memory. We always take heaps of footage and photos throughout the day, so it's great to have them ready to go the night before.

Invoke the Christmas Day rule

On Christmas Day the kids can eat anything they want, when they want for the entire day. My family love to have lots of treats on Christmas Day and it had become tiresome to keep track of what the kids were eating. It surprised me how restrained the kids can be. They also know Boxing Day is detox day and that it's back to healthy eating again.

Be flexible with routines

It can be incredibly difficult to take a toddler away from family, toys and food for an afternoon nap. In recent years, I've let the toddler fall asleep on my lap as I sit and talk with family. Or, other times, I've let them keep going and put them to bed an hour or two earlier at the end of the day. Either way, increasing my flexibility increased the enjoyment of the day for both of us.

Keep it simple, nice, easy food and a game of backyard cricket (with some champagne). All my kids care about at the table are the Christmas crackers!

Natasha Key, mum of three

Taking action

- Begin making preparations for Christmas in July when things are quieter.

- Choose a theme for your Christmas to simplify and coordinate Christmas festivities.

- In the months before Christmas (July to October) begin making some simple gifts for friends and family.

- Create a 10-week Christmas-preparation plan to spread the workload.

- To make catering easier, make a detailed Christmas Day menu plan.

- From the menu plan create a Christmas cooking schedule to highlight what you can do in advance.

- Delegate tasks to others to lighten your workload.

- Remember to get some rest and be flexible so everyone can enjoy the day—including you!

Final thoughts

There are moments in life that we remember vividly, regardless of how long ago they were. The emotions, the setting, the taste and the sound—all markers of a particular time in our life. For me, one of those moments was my husband, Phil, and I sitting in our rented house in Abbotsford at our tiny dining table eating pasta mixed with a jar of pesto, a glass of wine in hand, listening to a Wedding, Parties, Anything CD. It was nine o'clock at night and we'd just settled our first-born to sleep. We wondered in awe how parents with several children managed to eat a decent meal at a reasonable hour.

Now Phil and I only eat together on weekends, but it's with our lovely brood of five kids and it's generally at 5.30 pm, with a diet cola or a beer. It would be an understatement to say that we've learned much since that night 12 years ago. Parenting does get easier with experience. You become wiser, find shortcuts and develop strategies for coping with the daily toil required when caring for a young family.

Throughout this book I've illustrated the ways we streamline repetitive daily tasks so that not only can we get a meal on the table, but we also have more time for fun. It's been through using a planned approach that we've been able to grow our family, achieve personal goals and keep harmony in the home. We still do have moments of mess, fighting and tears, but planning has made managing these moments easier and less frequent.

What I've shared is the practical experience accumulated from my parenting journey to date. We didn't plan our life like this from the start. It took us time to find our feet, and to work out how we wanted to parent and how we could organise ourselves to do it to the best of our ability. It's with gradual steps that we make changes to our daily life so we can spend more time being with the kids, rather than doing for the kids.

If you haven't taken a planned approach to family life before, it's never too late to start. Keep it simple, start small and focus on the basics.

- Build routines for your kids. They give kids stability and a base from which to grow their independence.

- Have a menu plan. Mealtime is a big part of family life. Streamline this task and you significantly reduce the stress levels every evening and free up more time.

- Plan time for yourself, your kids, your partner and most importantly plan time for fun!

It's possible to achieve a level of organised chaos in family life. You can plan for the known repetitive tasks so you can better cope with whatever surprises your kids throw at you. It doesn't have to take the spontaneity out of life, but planning can provide a solid foundation for you and your kids to take on new adventures. It's an investment in time that will have more than repaid itself by the time everything's done.

Wishing you and your family every happiness in your organised chaos.

Index

Index